Terry,

You ARE the Real Schmoozer! I Just Wrote the Book. All the Best my Brotha

Cocly

9/1/20

Advance Praise for *Schmooze*

"Only Cody Lowry can up your game with the wink of an eye. In *Schmooze*, this proven performer not only shares the secrets of his success, he shows you how, and why, to put your life on 'schmooze-control.'"

—ERIC O'KEEFE, Editor, *The Land Report*

~

"Having grown up with two immigrant parents who spoke Yiddish as their primary language, how could I be anything but extremely enthusiastic about this book? I was taught that if you want to succeed in life, you'd better learn how to schmooze…and to do it authentically. In *Schmooze*, Cody amplifies how 'we' are the key to our own happiness and shows us how to live a richer, more fulfilled, and less complicated life. I'm sure everyone will enjoy this entertaining read, and will be a much better person for having read it."

—SANDY SCHWARTZ, President, Cox Automotive

~

"When I met Cody, I immediately felt his schmoozing charm. This authentic, genuine individual could put a smile on the most difficult of guests. Simply put, the world needs more schmoozing and Cody delivers."

—RAFFAELE RUGGERI, CEO, Bice Restaurant Group
(15+ Worldwide Locations)

SCHMOOZE

What They *Should* Teach at
Harvard Business
School

CODY LOWRY

SAVIO
REPVBLIC

A SAVIO REPUBLIC BOOK
An Imprint of Post Hill Press
ISBN: 978-1-64293-515-8
ISBN (eBook): 978-1-64293-516-5

Schmooze:
What They Should Teach at Harvard Business School
© 2020 by Cody Lowry
All Rights Reserved

Cover Design by Chief Mojo
Illustrations (Caricatures) by Jeff York

This is a work of nonfiction. All people, locations, events, and situations are portrayed to the best of the author's memory.

posthillpress.com
New York • Nashville
Published in the United States of America

For My 11 Grandchildren...

Number Nine, Elisha, not shown.
She is waiting for all of us in Heaven.

Table of Contents

Acknowledgments.. ix

Foreword by Dr. Nido Qubein.. xi

Author's Note xiv

Chapter One   *Schmoozing* Early 17

Chapter Two   Say Cheese.. 27

Chapter Three   Chutzpah.. 39

Chapter Four   Be a Contrarian 55

Chapter Five   Call Me Crazy.. 69

Chapter Six   *Schmoozing* on the Links................................ 87

Chapter Seven   The "What-If" Syndrome.............................. 101

Chapter Eight   The Spoils of *Schmoozing* 121

Chapter Nine   *Schmoozing* from the Podium 135

Chapter Ten   *Schmooze* Essentials.. 151

About the Author.. 173

Acknowledgments

There is nothing casual about writing a book, and maybe with few exceptions nobody does it alone.

I am so grateful to many people who helped mold my personality at an early age, including my Uncle Fred, who was a bigger than life ad guy from Detroit, Michigan. When he walked into any room, the world stopped, and the stage belonged to him. As you will soon learn in this book, there's a lot more to *schmoozing* than idle chit chat…it's about being there for people who are struggling or just down on their luck. For the last years of his life, my Uncle Fred, a recovering alcoholic, belonged to Alcoholics Anonymous, where he worked with other alcoholics, helping them find sobriety in their own lives.

Thank you to my brother-in-law Allen Pusey, formerly with the *Dallas Morning News* and past editor and publisher of the *American Bar Association Journal*, whose early praise and encouragement were instrumental in getting me out of the starting blocks with a big bolt of confidence.

Thank you to my siblings: Mimi, Mac, and Mike, who also weathered the childhood storm and all its craziness.

Thank you to some of my fellow *schmoozers*, friends, and business colleagues who have had an impact on my life and could all write their own *Schmooze* Manual: restaurateur Malio Iavarone, hotelier Bruce Dunbar, my favorite bartender and a great family man James Brisco, and three very successful automobile dealers with personalities and hearts bigger than their dealerships—Greg

York, Len Nadolski, and Bob Elliott. To my attorney and lifelong friend Richard Salem, whose ability to overcome blindness has been a great inspiration in my life, and to national speaker and South Florida icon, TV news and sports personality Tony Segreto.

Thank you to my cheerleaders, whose genuine interest and continuous prodding to finish the book over the last two years has kept me motivated: Dr. Stanley Schrum, Buddy Register, Alen Maric, Everette Atwell, Jose Terry, Eric Kennedy, Flavio Galasso, and my twenty-year sidekick and business associate, who I think memorized every chapter, Clark Wichman.

Thank you to my devoted assistants who kept the i's dotted and the t's crossed: Shea Posey and Brooke Lowry, as well as four immensely helpful creative professionals in John Samaha, Cordes Owen, Doug Blackmer, and Dan Mockensturm.

Thank you to author and publisher of the *Land Report*, Eric O'Keefe, whose mentoring and intimate knowledge of the publishing business proved to be invaluable.

And a special thanks to Jan Miller, Austin Miller, and Nena Madonia from the Dupree Miller Agency, and to Debra Englander and Heather King of Post Hill Press.

Finally, and most importantly, thank you to the "A" team: my wife Phyllis, Marnie, Cody Jr., Chelsea, and Kipp.

Cover Design—the Mojo Ranch, Clearwater, Florida

Caricatures—Jeff York, Chicago, Illinois

Foreword by Dr. Nido Qubein

Cody Lowry never shrinks from a challenge.

He's portrayed a pirate at a local amusement park, worked as a stand-up comedian and impressionist, auditioned for *Saturday Night Live*, and run a marathon after he heard his friend say, "Cody, you can't run a marathon. That's 26.2 miles."

He used a cheesecake to seal a meeting with President Jimmy Carter in 1976, carried the torch for the 2002 Winter Olympics, and helped coax the Vatican to have Pope John Paul II sign a baseball for his friend, Sparky Anderson, the legendary baseball manager.

I've known Cody for a long time, and he can tell these stories well. But I've often wondered how this genius marketer and respected advertising executive has had the chutzpah to pull it all off.

Now I know. You'll know too. The answer is in your hands— *Schmooze: What They Should Teach at Harvard Business School.*

The title is appropriate. Cody definitely has earned a PhD in *schmooze*. As he says in his book, "When you're 75 percent Irish, you're pretty good at blah-blah-blah speak."

Cody is more than "pretty good." He has a gift. He motivates with a smile, gives from the heart, and believes in the power of can-do optimism. He follows these three steps with everything he does: build a relationship, get people to trust you, and never let them down.

It sounds simple. It's not. Just look around us.

We don't talk to one another. We tend to look at our phones rather than look someone in the eye. Our technology has made us the most connected society in human history, and yet we've become more disconnected because of it.

Technology, mind you, is not bad. But we depend on it so much today that we're forgetting why we need face-to-face communication in the first place. We need to connect. It is crucial to who we are.

That's why *Schmooze* is so important. Cody shows us in a very entertaining, engaging way how *schmooze* has helped him—and how it can help all of us.

He gives us a road map we all can follow. We'll be less fearful, more caring, and more daring with our dreams, and we'll see chance encounters as opportunities to learn, lead, and be who we want to be.

We all want that.

At High Point University, I teach a life-skills seminar every year to our first-year students, and I tell them to believe in "the art of the possible." I want them to know that they can do whatever they dream as long as they work smart, work hard, and work their vision.

But they also must understand the importance of saying "please" and "thank you." They need to listen twice as much as they talk, and they need to know that service is the rent they'll pay for occupying a space on our Earth.

When I see the puzzled looks, I tell them that our value to humanity depends on how much of ourselves we give to make the world a better place.

Cody has done just that.

In *Schmooze*, Cody shows us through his many humorous stories how he has built his brand, remained a lifelong learner, and taken calculated risks that have paid off.

Meanwhile, we see on more than a few pages how an old Japanese proverb has become his philosophy for life: Fall down seven times, get up eight.

Cody does believe in the impact of what I call "relational capital." I tell our students that "relational capital" is one of the most important lessons they'll learn. It boils down to this: people don't know you care until you show them how much you care.

Cody does care. That theme is a common thread throughout the ten chapters in *Schmooze*. We see a grace in how Cody treats people—from a homeless stranger to a Super Bowl coach.

It's not about giving back. It's just about giving. That's it. Giving. Cody knows it is simply the right thing to do.

So, read *Schmooze*. You'll laugh, for sure. But you'll definitely learn how a former paperboy from South Florida went from hawking newspapers outside Nick's Bar to becoming a husband, father, grandfather, mentor, and successful businessman.

"Look," Cody writes, "I know everyone wasn't born with a lamp shade on their head, but you can still make a conscious decision to start each day with a little laughter in your life. Remember, if you live to be a hundred, life is still short, so have fun!"

True.

Nido R. Qubein
President
High Point University
High Point, NC

Author's Note

The word *schmooze* comes from the Yiddish word *shmuesn*, which means to "chat idly" or "to chat in a friendly and persuasive manner, especially so as to gain favor in business, or connections."

For me, someone who has walked the walk, *schmooze* has taken on a much broader definition. It's been a way of life. It's about thinking outside the box. It's about having fun and developing a sense of humor, and then using that humor to enrich the lives of others. It's about being genuine when there's nothing to gain. It's about building relationships, having a winning smile, and making a great first impression. It's about being persistent and overcoming adversity. It's about selling yourself. It's about thinking big and about being kind to all, regardless of class. In short, *schmooze* is about succeeding in life with a great "bedside manner."

In this book, I've tried to showcase how the aforementioned definitions of *schmooze* have been instrumental in a better life for me, and how you might easily adapt and apply them in your own life. Do I really believe they should teach *schmooze* at Harvard? Absolutely! And every other college too, for that matter.

We all know people from various walks of life, including very successful, highly educated people who, for whatever reason, seem to be miserable. They live in the "me" moment. They go through life with their chin in their chest, and they live in a world where the glass is half empty. The good news is that it's not too late for them, and even they can start charging in a better direction!

So, sit back, put your mind-set on *schmooze control*...and enjoy the ride!

Chapter One

SCHMOOZING EARLY

"Be kind whenever possible. It is always possible."

— Dalai Lama

I wasn't born with a golden spoon in my mouth, but as best as I can determine, my family was pretty well off. My mother and father both came from good stock. My mother's father, Frank Cody, was a successful politician in Detroit. From 1919 to 1946, Dr. Cody was superintendent of schools in Detroit, and he was appointed the first president of Wayne State University in 1933. In addition to his educational achievements, my grandfather was always a welcome guest at the podium and quite a humorist in his own right. When there was a controversy over how long teachers' skirts should be, he said, "I can't tell how long they should be until I have a look at the teacher." (Not the most politically correct answer by today's standards.) One quote that I love best and, as it relates to this book, I believe really fits is, "Algebra is an important study, but not nearly as important as knowing how to meet and mingle with people." Dr. Cody stayed active in education until he was seventy-two. In 1955, a high school in Detroit was dedicated to him, and it still stands today—Frank Cody High School.

My life on easy street didn't last very long. By the time I was five years old, my family (Mom, Dad, older sister Mimi, older brother Mac, and younger brother Mike) had moved to South Florida. And boy, did we move! In fact, we moved to so many places it's hard to remember them all. Within a seven-year period, and about a seven-mile radius, we moved thirty-two times. We actually lived in two places twice, which probably makes sense, because there was only so much rental property available within that seven-mile radius. I can remember walking home from school with my little brother Mike one day, and guess what? We didn't live there anymore. Think about that. You wake up in the morning, go off to school, and six hours later, there are locks on the door! Another time, we moved the day after Christmas. My mom was so upset (who wouldn't be?). She kept asking my father, "What about the Christmas tree? What about the Christmas tree?" After about three requests, my father ran into the house, grabbed the tree—ornaments, lights, tinsel (remember tinsel?), everything—and threw it into the back of an open pick-up truck. My dad had a lot of talents, but paying the rent wasn't one of them.

From that point on, I could fill in the blanks with all the craziness that goes along with this incredibly inauspicious start: the alcoholism, the lights being turned off, the government food (Spam and peanut butter…yummy!), being the only Cub Scout in the pack without a uniform, a violent papa, and a whole lot more. But because this book is not meant to be a catharsis on a wonderful childhood, I'll focus on *schmoozing* early.

As bad as it was, I can remember my mother staying positive and instilling a sense of pride and better times to come in my siblings and me. We all entered the workforce at an early age. For me, it was at age eleven when I became a full-fledged paperboy for the *Miami News*. At the time, there were two newspapers in Miami, the *Miami News* and the *Miami Herald*. For sure, the *Herald* was the dominant paper, but at least the *News* had a following in my hometown of Fort Lauderdale.

My beat was the Sunrise Center (today the Galleria), which at the time was one of the most upscale shopping centers in South Florida. One of the perks of the job was a brand-new canvas change bag that wrapped around my waist. (I was really proud of that new bag!) So, after school, I would head over to the shopping center to meet my boss, who would give me fifteen papers to sell over a three-hour period. On Saturdays, I would arrive at the shopping center around 10 a.m. and would have thirty papers to sell. I got a whopping two cents for every paper sold. Even at age eleven, I knew I would have to rely on tips to make any money at all. Obviously, back then, the word *schmooze* was not part of my vocabulary, but this I did know: if I wanted to sell all my papers, I had to hustle. And hustle I did. I walked the full length of the mall three or four times, hawking my papers to anyone and everyone I encountered.

"*Miami News*, ma'am…*Miami News*, sir? This is the Blue Street Edition, ma'am, the day's latest news!" Of course, most of the people I approached didn't want the *Miami News* and could've cared even less that I had the Blue Street Edition. One of my fondest memories was selling papers to Lillie Rubin, one of fashion's grand dames of the time. She had a high-end dress shop across the street on Sunrise Boulevard. I liked Mrs. Rubin, and I knew she really liked me. Every day, I would make a beeline to her store, and if she was there, she'd buy a paper. The nice thing about Lillie Rubin was that she always gave me a quarter for a five-cent newspaper.

While I didn't know it at the time, I was learning some pretty good life lessons, as well as getting some valuable sales experience. One takeaway I learned early on was that "no" didn't necessarily mean "no." One *schmooze* tactic that really worked like a charm was my response if someone said "no." As they walked by me in a hurry to get to wherever they were going, the last thing most of these people wanted was the *Miami News* (even if it was the Blue Street Edition). "Paper, sir?…Paper, ma'am?" And as they rushed by, most ignoring me, I would scream out in a voice at least two octaves higher than my normal, "Would you buy a paper if I told you where you got your shoes…what state you were born in… and how many birthdays you've had?" This would make some of the busiest people in South Florida stop dead in their tracks. They would turn around, usually with a big smile on their face, and give me the go-ahead. "You got your shoes on your feet…you were born in the state of infancy…and you've only had one birthday— the day you were born!" Anyone who took the bait always bought a paper and, more times than not, had a pretty good laugh. There was, however, an exception to that pretty good laugh that I will never forget.

On Saturdays, I usually sold my thirty papers, but it wasn't easy. You see, I never wanted to go home with any papers left, so I would work until it was almost dark. One Saturday morning, my manager announced that because I could sell thirty papers, he wanted me to sell fifty papers that day. I remember thinking at the time that there was no way I could sell fifty papers. Well, after a little encouragement and a pat on the back from my manager, off I went, determined to do what no paperboy had ever done before: sell fifty papers in one Saturday at the Sunrise Center. That day, I pitched every breathing, walking person. I approached some people twice, forgetting that I'd already pitched them. Unfortunately, it started to get dark, and I still had twelve papers left. I was dead tired. I had two options if I wanted to go home without any papers. One option was to go to Nick's Bar. This somewhat upscale bar was in a professional building adjacent to the shopping center. Nick was a great guy with his own PhD in *schmooze*. He would see me and scream out, "Hey, kid, give me a paper!" Then he would do something very special—he'd start hawking my papers to his patrons. Sometimes he wouldn't even get the name of the paper right. "Who wants a *Herald*?" Nobody really cared, and I'd usually end up walking out with most of my papers sold.

My other option was to go across the street to Wolfe's, a Jewish delicatessen on the corner just two doors down from Lillie Rubin's. Because it was closer, that's where I decided to go. So, I ran across the busy Sunrise Boulevard, only to be terribly disappointed. There, in front of Wolfe's, was a grown man selling the early edition of the *Miami Herald*. At the time, I'm sure the Sunday *Herald* was bigger than the *New York Times*. That Sunday paper had to be about three inches thick, loaded with news, sports, weather, and every imaginable advertising insert. This guy had three stacks of papers that reached the top of the overhang in front of the restaurant. Now think about it…here was this guy selling the early edition of the Sunday *Herald*, and here I was selling the Saturday morning *Miami News*, a paper one-twentieth the size of the *Herald*. At age eleven, I couldn't have been very smart, because the rational thing to do would've been to head over to Nick's Bar and take my chances there.

Instead, I dug in my heels, and much to the chagrin of the man selling the *Herald*, started hawking the *Miami News*. I was positioned right in front of the door, no more than ten feet away from the *Herald* stand, and almost everyone walking out got an aggressive invite to buy the *Miami News*. "*Miami News! Miami News!* Blue Street Edition!" To anyone observing, it must have been somewhat laughable. The *Herald* was selling so fast, the guy didn't have to say a word. And even with my enthusiastic pitch, I couldn't get a second look. I had been standing out there for fifteen to twenty minutes, and because it was already dark, I decided to take my papers and head home. As I was collecting my papers, a guy came blowing out of the restaurant, obviously in a bit of a hurry. Instinctively, I screamed out, "*Miami News*, sir?" He didn't turn around, so I started moving in his direction and with my last gasp of the day, I screamed out, "Sir, would you buy a paper if I told you where you got your shoes, what state you were born in, and how many birthdays you've had?"

He turned around so abruptly, I thought he was going to hit me. He sure didn't look happy, and I must've been a sorry sight. I was covered with newspaper ink—on my hands, on my face, all over my shirt. My change bag was no longer nice and tidy, hanging low, and turned to the side. I'm sure I needed a haircut too. Simply put, I looked a little like the Artful Dodger who needed a good bath. Well, this guy looked down at me and, unlike so many customers I'd had that day, was *not* smiling, but in a soft, compassionate voice that didn't match his initial look, he said, "Son, how many papers do you have left?" I replied, "I have twelve, sir." To which he responded, "That's exactly how many papers I want, and then I want you to go home!" That was an act of kindness that this eleven-year-old really needed and appreciated at the time. To this day, when I think of that moment, it still brings a tear to my eye.

Wouldn't it be great if we were all big-time philanthropists and we had the resources to donate large sums of money to charities, colleges, foundations, and the like? Just think of the impact we could have on the lives of a multitude of needy and worthy people everywhere. Just think of how good that would make us feel. Well, guess what? You don't need to give to the multitudes to feel good and make a difference in the lives of others. Every day, we cross paths with people a whole lot less fortunate than the general public as a whole. People who are down on their luck, people who, for whatever reason, don't look or act like us.

Several years ago, I was in Rome on a ten-day vacation with my wife and our parish priest, Father Caulfield. That day, my wife wasn't feeling well, so Father and I were taking in some sights. As we were walking by the Pantheon, I saw something I almost couldn't believe. There was a man panhandling in the street. Not so unusual, I know, but this man was different. He had no arms, no legs…just a torso on a thin piece of wood with what looked like roller-skate wheels. I stood there for several minutes in total disbelief. It wasn't his physical condition that gave me pause, but rather the fact that, as he lay there begging, he was for the most part ignored by almost everyone. Here in this very busy corridor in Italy, with a flow of people like a carnival, lay a very lonely person.

This man was totally ignored by most, and when someone did put something in his can, they did it without any human interaction (leaning down, dropping their donation, and then off they went). When Father and I approached him, I leaned down and, with a smile on my face, said, "*Ciao!*" (about the only Italian word I knew). The man lit up like a Christmas tree! I was *schmoozing*, and he was *schmoozing* back. We spent some time with this man and, while we didn't speak the same language, we didn't have to. We connected. When we were ready to leave, Father blessed him, I put some money in his can, we said our goodbyes (*Ciao*, once again), and turned and walked away. I hadn't taken ten steps when I turned to get one last look at my new friend. He was zeroed in on me like a laser, and he had a great big goodbye smile on his face, so I returned the gesture with a big goodbye smile of my own.

In the fast-paced daily grind that so many of us are exposed to, we encounter people that need a little human interaction. They need just a little kindness and to see that look in your eye that lets them know you really care.

In his book *Why Kindness Is Good for You*, Dr. David R. Hamilton cites a study in which 122 random people were given a flower. Everyone responded positively, with women responding a little more positively than men. The study pointed out that in our modern, fast-paced society, people have learned to look out mostly for themselves, and not so much for others. Hamilton wrote that this has become such a routine that we have forgotten to be kind to strangers for the sheer pleasure of helping a fellow human being.

I believe American-British author Henry James, considered by many to be among the greatest novelists in the English language, nailed it when he said, "Three things in human life are important: the first is to be kind; the second is to be kind; and the third, is to be kind."

The Takeaway

Remember, it's how you treat the less fortunate when nobody is looking that matters! Some might remember the 1985 AT&T advertising campaign, "Reach out and touch someone." My advice—do it today. It might make their day, and it will for sure make yours.

Chapter Two

SAY CHEESE

*"We shall never know all the good that
a simple smile can do."*

— MOTHER TERESA

The late Andy Rooney, best known for his weekly broadcast of "A Few Minutes with Andy Rooney" on *60 Minutes,* once said, "If you smile when nobody else is around, you really mean it." Well, that's exactly what I'm doing right now. I'm sitting on a plane headed to Greensboro, North Carolina, working on this chapter, and I have this incredible smile on my face. In fact, I'm almost giddy. I'm thinking of a larger-than-life person who had a profound influence on my brother and me. His name was Hugh Hoffman, and the very thought of this incredible person evokes some of the most wonderful adolescent memories anyone could have. His advice and fatherly counsel at that time in my life instilled a sense of confidence in me that I don't believe I would have otherwise had.

When I was growing up, *Reader's Digest* was the best-selling consumer magazine in the country. From time to time they would feature stories in their "The Most Unforgettable Character I Ever Met" series. I often thought that one day I would have the opportunity to tell the story of this truly unforgettable character. Yes, Hugh was unforgettable, and he radiated *schmooze.*

The first thing one noticed upon meeting Hugh Hoffman was not his size, even though he stood at six feet, four inches and weighed about 234 pounds. He had these incredibly large features—big hands, big feet, big ears, a big nose, and a head that was so big it almost looked disproportionate to the rest of his body.

No, the first thing I noticed, as I'm sure most people did, was his unbelievable smile. Hoffman's smile stretched almost from ear to ear, and when you encountered him, or whenever he walked into a room, that smile was contagious because everybody else couldn't help but smile with him.

My first recollection of meeting Hugh (as we called him, rather than Mr. Hoffman) was with my younger brother Mike, who actually had met him first. By this time, my dad was long gone, and who knows...maybe we were searching for a father figure to fill the void. Hugh was a tax accountant who lived in my hometown of Fort Lauderdale. His small, modest home behind Fort Lauderdale High School was also his office, and at first blush you would have thought that this guy couldn't have been very successful, which would've been a bad observation, because he was, in fact, very successful. He had made a fortune in the stock market. As I recall, his big home run was buying IBM stock when nobody else had bought IBM stock. He also did incredibly well with his tax accounting business. He was a voracious reader, well versed on almost any topic, especially politics and current events. If you ever got into a debate with him, you'd better know your facts, because there was a good chance that he knew your side of the argument better than you did.

In addition to that great big *schmooze* smile of his, Hugh was a master at giving advice. He always tried to steer my brother and me in the right direction with what we called *Hoffmanisms*:

> "Cody, when the maid comes over, I hide money in the seat because it tells me two things. One, if she's honest...two, if she cleaned there."

> "Cody, you never lend money to a friend. It's the quickest way to lose one."

He never gave my brother or me a dime but would let us do chores for him even if he had to make up the work. I remember the day I wanted to make a little extra money for homecoming. I went to his office to see if he had any jobs that I could do. This was a tough question for him to answer because it didn't appear that he had anything for me to do. He finally said, "OK, mow the lawn." When I said it looked like somebody had just mowed it, he yelled back, "Well, mow it again!"

Then there was the time when I was in college and driving a really old car. It felt like it used more oil than gasoline. The brakes were absolutely shot, and because I knew that I had a tax refund of $150 coming to me, I figured Hoffman would surely advance me the money. (He would do my taxes for free, and any refund I had coming would be sent to his office address.) Well, when I got to his office, he was slammed. He had one person in his office with three more in the waiting area. I did what I always did and walked straight into his office. As busy as he was, he took the time to greet me and then introduced me to his client, bragging about how someday I was going to be very successful.

"Cody," he said, "come back after six and we'll play some chess."

"Hugh, I need to talk to you," I told him.

"Not now," he said, "I'm too busy."

"Hugh, I need just a minute."

"Cody, you can see I'm busy," he said, as he turned his chair around and resumed the talk with his client.

So, I gave it one more try. "Hugh, I need to talk to you."

With that, he turned his chair towards me, looked at his watch, and without taking his eyes off his watch said, "You have one minute!"

I said, "Hugh, I have to borrow some money."

He then threw his hands up in the air and proclaimed, "Well, I guess that ends that conversation!" He immediately turned his chair back around. By that point, I wasn't upset. In fact, I was mildly amused. This was vintage Hoffman at his best. Of course, he was thinking what I was thinking—*never lend money to a friend*.

Interrupting once again, I said, "Mr. Hoffman, the brakes went out on my car. I need to get them fixed. I can pay you back with my tax refund." Once again, he turned his chair around, and I'll admit I was a little surprised as to what came next. "OK," he said, as he pulled out a promissory note from one of his files and began filling in the blanks, including the amount of the one hundred dollars that I needed. He signed the contract, I signed the contract, and even his client, who was now the witness to this high-priced transaction, signed the contract. On the surface, one might get the impression that Hugh was tight or cheap, but nothing could've been further from the truth. On the contrary, he was incredibly generous.

In the early '60s, Hugh founded Religious Vacations Inc., which offered a week-long vacation in Fort Lauderdale to hundreds of preachers and clergy and their families from all over the United States. They would stay in one of four Religious Vacation homes that he purchased and maintained. Religious Vacations Inc. was more than Hugh's avocation; it was his passion. For the most part, the homes stayed booked year-round, but when there was the occasional cancellation, he would get so upset because there was a good chance that he had turned down another family for that time slot. As a man who declared on many occasions that he had read the Bible cover to cover three times, Hugh was really in his element when those preachers came to town.

Upon arrival, they would be greeted by Hugh and that big *schmooze* smile of his. He would give them the lay of the land and tell them what sites to see during their visit to Fort Lauderdale. On many occasions, I went with Hugh to meet the families, and almost always, he'd work in a different and relevant Bible verse that I had never heard.

For sure, Hugh Hoffman was not cheap. He bought both my high school and college rings, neither of which I had the money for. And, even as I grew older and could well afford to pick up a check, he always beat me to the draw.

Another *Hoffmanism*? If somebody initiates the bet, don't take it. About two years transpired after those great words of wisdom were bestowed on me before I had an opportunity to put them into practice. What happened was very funny. I had stopped by Hoffman's office one day, and out he came, saying, "Cody, I just picked up my new Cadillac today and I'll bet you one dollar and will give you one minute to find the horn on my new car. And let me warn you, four people have already lost today." I immediately remembered his advice, "If somebody initiates the bet, don't take it!" With that in mind, I hardly gave his proposition any thought at all and immediately changed the subject. After a couple of minutes, he headed back into his office, giving me the opportunity to fully take advantage of the situation. I used his phone in the waiting area to call Connor Brown Cadillac, which was then Fort Lauderdale's only Cadillac dealership. When the salesman got on the phone, I politely asked where the horn was in the new Cadillac. "Oh," he said, "all you do is squeeze the steering wheel."

"That's it?"

"That's it—just squeeze the steering wheel," he repeated. I hung up and started laughing so hard that I could barely compose myself, knowing the fun I was about to have. When Hugh came out of his office, I immediately inquired about the horn and his new Cadillac. Oh boy, there was that smile, and I could tell he was excited about reeling in his next pigeon! "I'll bet you one dollar and I'll give you one minute to find the horn on my new car," he wagered once again. Then, being the gentleman that he was, he reminded me, "Four people have already lost today."

"OK, Hugh, I'll take that bet."

He was so excited—almost like a kid. We went out to his new Cadillac and I got into the driver's seat. The window was down, and my hands were on the steering wheel, and as I looked up at Hugh, he was focused on his watch. You'd have thought it was some sort of a shuttle launch. "Don't go yet…don't go yet…alright, ready…set…go!" He hadn't completely gotten through the word *go* when I immediately squeezed the steering wheel. "*Son of a bitch!*" he exclaimed. Hugh was in utter shock and, on this very rare occasion, wasn't smiling. But, as he stood there in total disbelief, his smile started to return, and he began to give me the respect and high praise that I rightly deserved, saying, "I should have known a smart young man like you could have figured it out." Of course, I didn't want to disappoint those wonderful thoughts by explaining just how this smart young man really figured it out, so it was probably a year later when I told him the whole story…and he loved it!

One of my fondest memories of Hugh and that great big smile happened years after his mentoring of my adolescence in Fort Lauderdale. I was living in what is now my hometown of Lakeland, Florida, about a four-hour ride from Fort Lauderdale. Uncle Hugh, as my kids called him, was coming for a visit, and we were all looking forward to his arrival, including five-year-old Cody Jr., four-year-old Chelsea, and three-year-old Kipp. The four of us were playing in the front yard, waiting for the big guy to arrive, when he came driving up in his substantial Cadillac sedan. The kids were excited, not just because it was Uncle Hugh, but because they could see what appeared to be balloons in the back seat. Sure enough, Hugh reached into the back seat and out came four big, helium-filled balloons. The kids were jumping up and down in front of this Paul Bunyan of a man, waiting for him to hand them a balloon. He gave one first to Cody Jr., then to Kipp. When he reached down to hand Chelsea her balloon, she saw an opportunity to get two balloons and tried to grab the fourth one. Hugh quickly stood up straight, holding the balloon high over his head, explaining to Chelsea in no uncertain terms that that was his balloon. I laughed because I knew Hugh was serious. This indelible Norman Rockwell moment with Hugh, the kids, their four balloons, and their four big smiles will never leave me.

Hugh Hoffman for sure did not teach me to smile, but there is no doubt that I learned from him the importance and the advantages of making a smile part of my repertoire. A smile is a way to disarm, to persuade, to influence, to connect, and to charm. But the best news of all…a smile is free, and it might even make you live longer. Ron Gutman, CEO of HealthTap, a company that specializes in free apps and online apps for health information, says that your smile isn't just a predictor of how long you could live, but that it also has a measurable effect on your overall well being. Mr. Gutman cites a 2010 Wayne State University research project that examined baseball card photos of major-league players in 1952. The study found that the span of a player's smile could actually predict the span of his life. Players who didn't smile in their pictures lived an average of 72.9 years, while those with beaming smiles lived to almost eighty.

Dr. Mark Stibich, who earned his PhD in health behavior from Johns Hopkins University, gives us ten reasons to make a conscious effort to smile every day.

1. **Smiling makes us attractive.** We are naturally drawn to people who smile. There is a real physical-attraction factor linked to the act of smiling.

2. **Smiling relives stress.** Stress can permeate our entire being and can really show up in our faces. When you are stressed, take time to put on a smile. You and those around you will reap the benefits.

3. **Smiling elevates our mood.** Next time you are feeling down, try putting on a smile. There's a good chance your mood will change for the better. Think of smiling like a natural antidepressant.

4. **Smiling is contagious.** How many smiles have been described as having the power to light up a room? While it is certainly a beautiful sentiment, it carries a hint of truth. Smiling not only has the power to elevate your mood, it can also change the moods of others and make things happier.

5. **Smiling boosts your immune system.** Smiling can also boost your overall health. The act of smiling actually helps the human immune system to function more effectively. In addition to taking precautions like washing your hands, why not try to prevent the cold and flu by smiling?

6. **Smiling lowers your blood pressure.** When you smile, there is a measurable reduction in your blood pressure. Give it a try if you have a blood pressure monitor at home. Sit for a few minutes, take a reading, then smile for a minute and take another reading while still smiling. Do you notice a difference?

7. **Smiling makes us feel good.** Studies have shown that smiling releases endorphins, natural painkillers, and serotonin. Not only do these natural chemicals elevate your mood, but they also relax your body and reduce physical pain. Smiling is a natural drug.

8. **Smiling makes you look younger.** Not only can smiling make you look more attractive, it can also make you look more youthful. The muscles we use to smile also lift the face, making a person appear younger. So instead of

opting for a face-lift, just try smiling your way through the day—you'll look younger and feel better.

9. **Smiling makes you successful.** Studies have shown that people who smile regularly appear more confident, are more likely to be promoted, and are more likely to be approached. Try putting on a smile at meetings and business appointments. You might find that people react to you differently.

10. **Smiling helps you stay positive.** Try this test: smile, then try to think of something negative without losing the smile. It's hard, isn't it? Even when a smile feels unnatural or forced, it still sends the brain, and ultimately the rest of the body, the message that "life is good!"

A chapter on smiling would be incomplete without me telling you about a special person I've been doing business with for over twenty-two years. His name is Horace McKinney, and he owns and operates the shoeshine stand at the Piedmont Triad International Airport in Greensboro, North Carolina. Whenever I get off the plane and start heading down the concourse, if I'm lucky, I'll run into Horace, who always acknowledges me with eyes wide open, a big genuine smile, and a greeting meant for a king: *"Co-Deee!"* I always return the enthusiasm and scream back, *"Horace!"* We stopped shaking hands years ago; instead we give each other a big hug. I wish I could package and sell to the world all of Horace's remarkable attributes.

In addition to his million-dollar smile, Horace is an incredibly positive person with the ability to impart great advice with the spontaneity of a trained psychologist. Horace has been a gift in my life, as I'm sure he is for hundreds of different travelers. If you ever find yourself at the Greensboro airport, make sure to stop by for a big smile, and say hello to Horace. You'll be glad you did!

The Takeaway

An authentic smile is a prelude to a happy life. It not only helps open doors, helps to make a great first impression, and sets a positive tone for any engagement, but it's also the first line of defense against a world that at times can be negative and jaded. In my opinion, after the iconic smile of the Mona Lisa, Mary Tyler Moore had one of the most memorable smiles of all time. It's been forty years since the *Mary Tyler Moore Show* was on TV and yet I can visualize the opening to that sitcom like it was yesterday. The theme song "Love Is All Around," written and performed by Sonny Curtis, opens with this question: Who can turn the world on with a smile? The answer to that question is pretty easy...*you*!

Chapter Three

CHUTZPAH

"It ain't bragging if you can do it."

— Dizzy Dean

Chutzpah (hoot-spuh) is another Yiddish word, and it means "supreme confidence, nerve, gall." Example: It took a lot of *chutzpah* to stand up to him the way she did.

Author and evangelist Guy Kawasaki humorously defines *chutzpah* as "calling up tech support to report a bug in your pirated software." My favorite example of *chutzpah* is "a young man kills both his parents and then throws himself on the mercy of the court because he's an orphan."

Many of us from time to time have been asked whom we would like to sit down and have a beer with. High on my list would be American lawyer, jurist, law professor, and author Alan Dershowitz. I have great admiration for this man, who, in addition to his incredible career, graduated number one in his class at Yale Law School and was the youngest full professor of law in the history of Harvard Law School at age twenty-eight. In his 1991 national bestseller *Chutzpah*, Mr. Dershowitz defines the word as "boldness, assertiveness, a willingness to demand what is due, to defy what is tradition, to challenge authority, to raise eyebrows." I would only add that I believe it's also about perseverance, acting on your beliefs, and doing what you know to be right without regard for wrath or negative consequences. In short, it's about "having a pair." Oh, and Professor Dershowitz, I'll buy the beer!

The entertainment industry is loaded with people who have *chutzpah*—people who didn't have an easy path to the top, who had doors closed in their faces, but who persevered because they believed in themselves. And they succeeded. Long before Sylvester Stallone was one of America's movie superstars, he was a struggling actor. Back in the early '70s, Stallone was living in a one-room Los Angeles apartment that was so small he could open the front door from his bed. He was so down and out that he actually sold his dog for $25 just so he could buy some food. During this time, he was inspired by a fight between Muhammad Ali and Chuck Wepner to write the iconic screenplay *Rocky*. The good news for Stallone was that the producers he pitched his screenplay to loved it. One stipulation for Sly was that he play the role of Rocky. Then came the bad news—the producers didn't want Stallone. They wanted Ryan O'Neal, Burt Reynolds, James Caan, or Robert Redford...anyone but Stallone to play the lead. He was originally offered $25,000, which he turned down. The producers kept upping their offer, finally getting to $375,000, and Sylvester Stallone still turned them down. If the movie was going to be made, Stallone was going to play the lead.

Now think about that. How many of us, including myself, without two quarters to rub together would turn down $375,000 (about $2 million in today's dollars)? That, my friends, is *Chutzpah*! *Chutzpah* with a capital *C*. The rest is history. Stallone went on to become one of the biggest box-office draws in the history of cinema. Incidentally, after signing the deal for the movie, Sylvester Stallone managed to buy his dog back, and that pup actually appeared in the movie!

When I graduated from the University of South Florida in Tampa, I was pretty proud of myself. Devoid of a parental checkbook, I finished in four years, only a few thousand dollars in debt. Financially, it wasn't always easy. An all-nighter for me was at times sleeping in my car. With that said, I only have fond memories of college, including the many part-time jobs I had. I was a waiter, a pirate at a local amusement park, even a worker at a J.C. Penney distribution center. I had many construction jobs, and during the college breaks (summer, spring, holidays), I always had a job thanks to a very special person. Dick Davis was the father of my very good friend, Mike Davis. Mr. Davis owned a large surveying and engineering company in Fort Lauderdale. I must say, the Davises, including Mr. Davis's beautiful bride, Jackie, always made me feel like I was just another member of the family. And it was a big family—the Davises had seven children of their own, along with two adopted daughters. During my high school years, there was always a seat for me at the dinner table. I remember thinking, "So this is what goes on in typical families." Even though the Davis family pretty much knew my family situation, I always tried to put up a good front. If I was at their house and it was getting late, I would jump up and say something like, "Oh wow, it's getting late! I'd better get home." I'd say it in a tone that gave the impression that I would get in trouble if I didn't hurry. Nothing could have been further from the truth. I could have stayed a week and that would've been just fine. Today, I look back on Mr. Davis as a guardian angel who was always there for me. If I needed to make a buck, all I had to do was call him, show up, and jump on a truck! Thank you, Dick Davis…RIP.

With my advertising and PR sheepskin in hand, I was ready to conquer the Tampa ad world. Unfortunately, the ad world wasn't exactly opening its arms to me. Finding a position took more time than I had—a lot more time than I had, because I was broke. I needed to start generating some cash flow.

What happened next, I owe to *chutzpah*. One night I was talking with my younger brother, Mike, who was going to school at the time and working part-time at a large Oldsmobile dealership in South Florida. He suggested that until I could find something in advertising, why not sell cars. I remember thinking, "He has got to be kidding!" I had just spent the last four years working my way through college, and I for sure was *not* going to sell cars. He then went on to tell me the kind of money I could make, and that they'd give me a new car to drive (demo). When he said "demo," that got my attention. Not only did I not have any cash, but the car I was driving was a 1963 Chevy Corvair, the car made famous by Ralph Nader's best-selling book *Unsafe at Any Speed*. Well, if it was unsafe when it rolled off the assembly line, it was for sure unsafe ten years later with 100,000-plus miles on it. A brand-new car to drive—that was all the encouragement I needed.

So, the very next day I started searching for a dealership where I would want to work. It didn't occur to me to look in the newspaper to see who might be hiring. My arrogance was in high gear, and I just knew that once I picked the dealership where I wanted to work, it would be a pretty simple process: they would meet me, love me, then hire me…and I would get a new demo. Well, it didn't exactly work out that way. I spent a day scouring the city in my clunker Corvair, searching and scoping out the new car dealerships in Tampa. At the end of the day, I had found my new temporary home—Roger Whitley Chevrolet, a new and modern Chevy store on the north side of town. Now that I had picked my new place of employment, there was only one thing left to do.

After driving by and observing some of the salesmen, it became clear that I needed a new wardrobe, or at least something I could wear to my interview. Those guys were some pretty flashy dressers. I had absolutely nothing that even came close to flashy, and I for sure didn't have any white shoes. (White shoes were definitely part of the uniform during that era.) So, with less than seventy-five dollars to my name, off I went to J.C. Penney to find some flashy digs for my big interview the next day. Of course, I was the only one who knew about the big interview. What I picked out was flashy indeed: baby blue pants, a white shirt, and a colorful paisley tie that matched my baby blue pants very smartly. I'm glad I didn't have enough money for shoes…I was really having a hard time envisioning myself in those white shoes.

So, there I was the next morning in my new duds, ready for my interview. I had a hard time sleeping the night before because all I could think about was my new Chevrolet demo. When I walked into the dealership, I went to the front desk and told the receptionist what I was there for. She made a call to the manager, and I was directed to Mr. Bucky Van DeBoe's office. So far, everything was going according to plan. When I walked into Bucky's office, I started to lose some of my confidence. There was no welcoming, glad-to-see-you smile, and in a remote corner of the office was another guy leering at me. He was seated in a chair and looked like a character at the Cantina in *Star Wars*. And, yes, you guessed it, he was wearing white shoes. Bucky, on the other hand, looked like the stereotypical car guy with his big, loud-colored sport coat with wide lapels. One thing that immediately stood out with Bucky was his hairdo. He didn't have one hair out of place, and that was probably because he used a whole can of hair spray that morning. He actually looked like he had a helmet on his head. I can't remember if we even shook hands, but what I do remember is feeling very uncomfortable. As I started to sit down, I began talking. "Mr. Van DeBoe, my name is Cody Lowry. I'm a recent graduate of the University of South Florida, and I want a career in the automobile business. I've researched almost every dealership in town, and this is where I would like to work…blah, blah, blah…." (When you're 75 percent Irish, you're pretty good at blah-blah-blah speak.!) When I was finished with my three-minute pitch to Bucky, without hesitation, he told me that they had just hired three new salesmen and to call back in three months. I was shocked! I was stunned beyond belief. He didn't want me to call back in three months… Bucky wanted me out of his life forever.

Suddenly, any confidence that may have left me earlier was back. I was exploding with confidence. I jumped out of my chair and looked down at Bucky and told him in a voice that I'm sure could be heard outside his office, "You just made one of the biggest mistakes of your life, because you don't have a salesman in this dealership that I can't outsell!" I quickly walked out of his office and through the front door. As I walked down the ramp in front of the door, out came the gentleman who had been sitting in the corner in Bucky's office. His name was Manny Fernandez, and it turned out that he was the truck manager.

As Manny was trying to catch up to me, I noticed he had a limp and a glass eye. With a big smile on his face, he said, "Cody! Cody, wait. I've never heard anyone talk to Bucky that way!" I replied with, "Bucky just made a big mistake." Manny was still smiling and said, "Look, I'm going to talk to Bucky. Give me a call around three today. Let me see what I can do." Just as directed, I called Manny back at three o'clock, and to my surprise he had talked to Bucky. I was to start the next morning. Wow! I wondered what color my demo would be.

At nine o'clock the next morning, I was standing in the show-room waiting on Manny. Because of my limited wardrobe, I was wearing the same baby blue pants, the same white shirt, and the same paisley tie. After a few moments, someone informed me that because Manny worked the night shift he wouldn't be in until noon, but that Mr. Van DeBoe was expecting me. Oh no, not Bucky again! I started to feel a little weak in the knees, so I took a deep breath and headed down to see my best friend Bucky.

When I walked into his office, he was sitting at his desk and appeared to be totally absorbed in his paperwork. In a bright, cheery, positive tone, I opened the meeting with, "Good morning, Mr. Van DeBoe!" Bucky, of course, exhibited the same charming personality he had exhibited the day before, and didn't answer me.

He didn't even look up. I took a seat in front of his desk and waited to be acknowledged. Several minutes went by and I decided to break the silence. "Mr. Van DeBoe, do you have a training class?" I asked. Bucky started to do something I didn't think he was capable of—he was smiling. In fact, he was smiling from ear to ear. Was I really that funny, or did it have something to do with my braggadocious proclamation the day before? All of a sudden, his smile turned into a scowl, and he asked me very directly if I could figure out 4 percent sales tax, to which I immediately answered in the affirmative. He then stood up from his desk and in a near scream told me to get out on "the point." Now, I didn't know where "the point" was, but I was pretty sure it wasn't in his office. I was also pretty sure they didn't have a training class. What I didn't know at the time was that Bucky and Manny had a little side bet going on as to how well I would do.

I got off to a rocky start, to say the least. This dealership had about twenty salesmen, and not a single one was glad I was there. They weren't friendly for a couple of reasons: One, I'm sure they were all aware of the side bet that was going on. And, two, the fact that I had told Bucky he didn't have anyone I couldn't outsell. For the first two days, I approached as many potential customers as I could. That did not sit well with the other salesmen. They accused me of taking all the "ups" (an "up" is a new customer on the lot), and I was probably guilty as charged. After almost two days, I hadn't sold a car, and even I was starting to think that maybe Bucky had been right.

On the evening of my second day, an elderly couple, Mr. and Mrs. Biamount (almost everyone remembers the name of their first customer), came to the dealership to buy a new Impala. There was nothing casual about the whole process of selling my first car. They looked at every Impala we had on the lot. They couldn't decide on the color…they couldn't decide on the equipment…they couldn't decide if they wanted cloth or vinyl. Then there was the trade-in. I don't think we could've ever given enough for the trade to please Mr. Biamount. After three hours, we still didn't have an agreement, so they asked Harry Cole, another salesman, to help close the deal. We eventually got on the same page as the Biamounts, and two days later they took delivery of their new Impala. When I received the wash-out sheet on my commission for the sale, that's when reality set in. Because it was a minimum deal, I got a flat commission of twenty-five dollars, but because I had to split it with Harry Cole, we both received only $12.50. The good news? My first full month selling cars, I led the board with twenty-four and half units sold. I guess Manny won that bet!

A quick word about Bucky. As you might expect, Bucky and I became very good friends. He really was a wonderful person and I give him a lot of credit for helping me jump-start my business career.

Incidentally, if you're right, use a little chutzpah and stand your ground. Several years ago, I flew into Columbia, South Carolina, on an evening flight. The plane was late, so by the time I got to the Marriott, it was almost 11 p.m. and I was dog tired. Before I go any further, let me say that I have stayed at Marriott hotels my entire business career, and on a scale of one to ten I would give them a 9.9. This night, however, they were off their game. When I walked into the lobby of the hotel, I couldn't believe the line waiting to check in. I thought I was at Disney World. It didn't take long for me to realize what was happening. The hotel had overbooked big time, and they were diverting everyone by way of shuttle to the Embassy Suites about a mile away. As I stood in line waiting my turn, I couldn't help but think how incredibly smart I was to have a confirmed, guaranteed reservation.

As other hotel guests bemoaned the fact that they had to go to a different hotel, I stood there with a smug grin on my face, knowing that shortly I would be upstairs and sound asleep in my confirmed, guaranteed hotel room. Well, after a thirty-minute wait, I stepped up to the counter ready to proclaim to the world and anyone else within earshot that I, Cody Lowry, the seasoned, smart, savvy road warrior, had a confirmed, guaranteed reservation. It didn't take long for me and my deflating ego to quickly realize that there was "no room in the inn," and that I was in fact destined for a road trip to the Embassy Suites. I wasn't going down without a fight, though, so I tried in vain to make my case to one of the front desk people.

I let him know right away that I was a Marriott Marquis customer who had a confirmed, guaranteed reservation. With a "big deal" look on his face, he let me know in short order that there were no rooms and that he would be happy to set me up at the Embassy Suites. I told him that that didn't seem fair to me. I then went on to tell him that had I not shown up that evening, the Marriott would've charged my credit card the cost of the room. It was at this point that my front desk *buddy* made a tactical error—he snapped at me (*snapped* is reserved for my wife alone). "Mr. Lowry, overbooking is something that happens with the airlines on a regular basis, and unfortunately that is our situation tonight." There was no doubt that with his inflection and aggravated tone, I quite clearly had just been snapped at. *Game on!*

"Young man, who's the general manager of this hotel?" I asked.

He replied, "He's not on tonight."

"Not the question I asked," I retorted. "Who is the general manager?"

He then yelled out a name that was obviously of German descent, but for sure not a common German name in America. I then asked him to spell it slowly so I could write it down, which he did, probably wondering what I was going to do. It was such a unique name that I knew if by any chance at all he had a listed number, I wouldn't have to guess at which one it was. I took a couple of steps back and called information on my cell phone for this particular name in Columbia, South Carolina. No sooner had I pronounced this very difficult name to the operator than she gave me the number. So, I started dialing. My front desk buddy was watching me closely. I knew he had to be thinking, "What kind of a nut would call somebody this late at night?!" Not only did I call my new German friend, but he answered the phone immediately. I began to tell my story, only this time with a new-found vigor because I believed I was right. After explaining my situation (can you say "guaranteed"?), I went on to explain that if he couldn't accommodate me tonight, I was prepared to track down Bill Marriott, or at least his assistant, and report what was occurring at one of his hotels. That parting shot was not just a threat.

This general manager knew I was prepared to follow through when I told him that there was no way I was leaving this hotel, and that I would sleep on one of the couches in the lobby if I had to. He immediately asked to speak to my front desk buddy. When I handed him my cell, I said, "Your boss wants to talk to you." He grabbed the phone and with a somewhat agitated voice said, "Yes, sir." Then in a lower tone, another "yes, sir." And yet again in a much lower voice, "Yes, sir." The last "yes, sir" was barely a whisper when he humbly handed me the phone. The next words out of his mouth surprised even me! "Mr. Lowry, we're going to put you in room 421."

"Perfect! Just the room I was looking for," I replied. Again, if you're right, make every effort to stand your ground!

Don't get me wrong. Exerting a little *chutzpah* now and then doesn't always have to be used in a contentious situation. In 1992, I was at the Orlando International Airport ready to get on a plane headed to Los Angeles in order to produce some commercials with popular radio and TV personality Art Linkletter for a local Buick dealer. Linkletter was the host on radio and TV for *House*

Party, which ran on CBS for twenty-five years, and *People Are Funny*, which ran on NBC for nineteen years. Perhaps Linkletter is best remembered for a segment in *House Party* called "Kids Say the Darndest Things." At the time, Linkletter was a young seventy-nine and the perfect demo and pitch man for the Buick buyer.

About thirty minutes before the plane was scheduled to take off, passengers were notified that an earthquake had just hit the city of Los Angeles. Everyone was given the option to either proceed as scheduled or to get a raincheck for another date. Few passengers opted out. When I arrived in L.A., you could immediately sense a tense concern and trepidation among the locals, and rightly so. This was no small earthquake. Measuring 7.4 on the Richter scale, it was one of the largest earthquakes to ever hit the city of Los Angeles.

When I arrived at the Marriott Marquis Marina del Rey, which was to be my home for the next two days, I was informed that because of structural damage as a result of the earthquake, I was being moved to the Ritz-Carlton Marina del Rey just a half a mile away (not a bad trade-off!). After checking in, and with time to kill, I decided to take a cab to Rodeo Drive, the shopping street of the rich and famous, where you can stroll by the same shops as Julia Roberts in *Pretty Woman*. Upon exiting my cab, it was immediately apparent that this Sunday afternoon—a time when this famous street should be bustling—was not going to be a big shopping day for the glitzy stores on Rodeo.

As I strolled down the street and by the shops and restaurants almost devoid of any people or activity, I walked into a men's clothing store named Bernini of Beverly Hills. This small boutique reeked of the upper crust and catered to a presumed social class that I was pretty sure I didn't belong to. I was the only customer, and as best as I could tell, only two other people were in the store—a young salesman and an older gentleman, who I later found out was the manager. As I perused the high-end fashions, I found one sport coat that I knew I just couldn't live without. That was until I saw the price. This wool and cashmere Hugo Boss gold and blue jacket had a price tag of $575 (today's price for the same quality coat would be north of $1,500). That was above my true-buy threshold by about $425. It was then that I noticed a 40 percent-off rack in the back of the store, and I strolled to it in hopes of getting a deal. As we all know, there's a good reason merchandise is deep-discounted, and it's usually because it's not very attractive and, more importantly, just not a big seller.

As I expected, there wasn't anything that interested me, and as I headed back to the front of the store to take one last look at the sport coat I would never own, the young salesman approached and asked if I wanted to try it on. Trying that coat on was the last thing I wanted to do, knowing that could very possibly be the beginning of a very long relationship with my new Hugo Boss. Instead, at that very moment, I decided to ask the young salesman if there was a chance that they would be willing to take 40 percent off this wool and cashmere coat. This seemed humorous to him a bit as he explained that that would not be possible. I didn't respond with a smile, but rather a straight face, and then asked the young man to at least ask his manager, who was on the phone at the time, if he would, as outrageous as it sounded, take 40 percent off the price of the coat. He stared at me for a moment with a "he's not kidding" look, then bravely turned around and headed for the back of the boutique to ask his manager if he was willing to accept my very generous offer. The manager, still on the phone, interrupted whoever he was talking to in order to listen to his salesman explain my unbelievable offer. It took only a matter of seconds to think it over, and with an expression that looked like he had just stepped into a pile of fresh horse manure, he gave the young man a back-handed wave as if to say, "Get rid of this guy and get yourself a real customer."

The problem with that thinking was that Bernini's was going to have a very, very slow day, and, who knows, I may have been their only customer. I thanked the young man and told him I would be in town for the next couple of days, and that I'd rethink the price and might be back. I had no intention of paying $575 for a sport coat. If the truth be known, 40 percent off was going to cost $345, still more than I could justify at the time. As I continued my stroll past the empty shops on Rodeo Drive, I didn't feel all that bad about not getting that coat. After all, as brash as my offer was, it may have been the only opportunity they'd had to sell something all day long. I was maybe two blocks down the street when I heard what I thought was someone screaming my name. When I turned around, the young man from Bernini's was running towards me, yelling, "Mr. Lowry! Mr. Lowry!" He was running so fast that when he finally reached me, he had to catch his breath. Then, with a smile on his face and maybe a sense of accomplishment, he said, "I told my boss that you probably wouldn't be back, and so he agreed to take 40 percent off the Hugo Boss you liked." Now think about that. I wasn't at some bargain outlet. I wasn't at a flea market. No, I was on what was arguably one of the ritziest shopping streets in the world, and because of the circumstances, they had agreed to my crazy offer. That coat is twenty-seven years old and just as fashionable today as it was in 1992. And to think, if I hadn't asked for 40 percent off, it would be hanging in someone else's closet today.

The Takeaway

Schmooze with a little *chutzpah* is a powerful combo that should be included in everyone's arsenal. *Chutzpah,* however, should be used with caution and in moderation. It should be a mind-set for the moment when you need to get your point across or if you're heading in a direction few would dare. Too much *chutzpah* and you run the risk of losing your relevancy and becoming someone to be avoided at all costs. When you take a look at highly successful people in business today, they almost always exhibit some sort of *chutzpah*. They're assertive. They're bold. They're gutsy. And, almost always, they exude a self-confidence that lets the world know, "I'm charging—time to move out of the way!"

Chapter Four

BE A CONTRARIAN

> *"If everyone is thinking alike,*
> *then somebody isn't thinking."*

> — GEORGE S. PATTON

Sometimes in life it's OK to be a contrarian, to go right when everyone else is going left. Too many times we let ourselves succumb to groupthink or the idea of "getting along by going along." Sometimes we need to throw caution to the wind, buck the system, and challenge the status quo. Our ideas and suggestions are often clouded by conventional wisdom that has run amok, when we'd be better served by acting on our instincts.

Fred W. Smith, founder and CEO of Federal Express, found himself in a situation that led him on one of the most unconventional paths in the history of modern business. In 1975, Federal Express was on the verge of bankruptcy. The company was losing over $1 million a month, and the banks had no interest in giving any additional loans. At its lowest point, FedEx had only $5,000 in the bank, which wasn't enough to continue buying fuel for its existing fleet of planes. So, what did Mr. Smith decide to do? He did the exact opposite of what most people of his business stature would ever consider doing—he flew to Las Vegas on a Friday and played Blackjack the whole weekend with the remaining company funds!

On Monday morning, to the shock of his management team, he deposited $32,000 in the company account, thereby giving him the capital needed to operate for a few more days. As it turned out, within those days, Mr. Smith managed to raise $11 million to keep the company running. Fred Smith was a contrarian, and it worked! And in 1976, Federal Express posted its first profitable year, with $3.6 million. (For what it's worth, in 2016 FedEx reported $1.82 billion net income...*Blackjack!*).

Another story of successful contrarianism happened in 1979. Still two years from opening my ad agency, I was working as the general new-vehicle manager at Abraham Chevrolet, a very large automobile dealership in Tampa, with about forty-five salespeople. By then, the only reason I was still in the car business was because of a very dynamic person—the dealer, Anthony Abraham. In addition to the Tampa dealership, he owned Anthony Abraham Chevrolet in Miami, which was advertised as the largest Chevrolet dealership in the country. On any given weekend, they would sell one hundred to 125 new and used vehicles. Mr. Abraham was a master at the podium. When he spoke, his audience was mesmerized. Incredibly articulate, Mr. Abraham always seemed to deliver the right message, with the right tone, with his own special cadence. He was so good that two of his iconic competitors—the Potamkins and the Bramans—would invite him to speak at their dealerships. One of Mr. Abraham's closest friends was actor Danny Thomas. Both were founding members of the St. Jude Children's Research Hospital. Over his lifetime, Mr. Abraham gave millions of dollars to St. Jude, and the Anthony R. Abraham Foundation is still giving to St. Jude to this day (as well as numerous other charities). Ironically, Mr. Abraham was also in the advertising business prior to getting in the automobile business. He owned an advertising agency headquartered in Chicago. The A&R Agency had offices around the country, including a New York office located in the Empire State Building.

At that time in 1979, Jimmy Carter's presidency was spiraling into an abyss. With an election just around the corner, inflation was at 12 percent, energy prices were soaring, and President Carter's approval rating dipped below 30 percent. Plus, he was heading into a wave of conservatism led by presidential candidate Ronald Reagan. With the mood of the country in the doldrums, Walter Annenberg (a Republican) felt the need to speak out in support of the president. Walter Annenberg was an American publisher (*TV Guide*), philanthropist, and diplomat. He was the U.S. ambassador to the United Kingdom from 1969 to 1974, and during his lifetime he gave away billions of dollars to various charities and foundations. On June 14, 1979, the *Chicago Tribune* featured an article written by Mr. Annenberg titled "The Summer of Discontent." The thrust of his article was this: as bad as most people felt about the condition of the country (a "crisis of confidence," some called it), the president needed our support—Jimmy Carter was our president, and he was the only one we had. After reading Annenberg's article, my boss, Mr. Abraham (also a Republican), decided to promote the message by running full-page, full-color patriotic ads in the *Miami Herald,* the *Tampa Tribune,* and the *St. Petersburg Times*, to the tune of about $20,000 (around $71K in today's dollars).

One day, news spread through the dealership that President Carter was coming to Tampa on Thursday, August 30. Later that same day, I was in a management meeting with Mr. Abraham's son, Tom, when I suggested that it would be nice if we could get a little publicity for the dealership by tying some event to the president's visit. "*Like what?*" was the question everyone was asking. I didn't know, so I said, "Let's think about it." Most everyone in the room said that there wasn't enough time, with just a little over a week before the visit, and they all agreed to move on to the next subject. That's when I spoke up and said, "Here's a thought…why don't we mount the Walter Annenberg article and present it to the president when he's in town?"

Everyone in the room thought I was nuts. One manager piped in with a laugh, "Hey...forget the president! Why don't you try to set up a meeting with the pope?" Even my buddy, Tom Abraham (still a very good friend today), laughed and thought setting up a meeting with the president in a week's time was almost impossible. Well, that was all the encouragement I needed. As everyone in the room headed left, I started heading right. Since there wasn't a how-to manual on setting up a meeting with the President of the United States with just one week's notice, I just followed my gut instincts and made a call to the office of the most high-profile person in the Carter administration, Jody Powell. Powell was not only press secretary in the Carter administration; he was in fact Jimmy Carter's closest advisor. So, that was my first call, and as I remember, it didn't last very long. I quickly found out that, as kind as everyone was through the whole process, they were not very forthcoming on how I could accomplish my mission (or maybe they just didn't know). They were, however, very good at passing me off to different offices.

So that's what happened. Secretary Powell's office referred me to another office, and that office sent me to yet another office, which then directed me to the president's scheduling office. The gentleman who answered could not have been nicer. He listened patiently to my enthusiastic pitch. I was persistent, but this guy had no idea who I was or what political connections I might've had (I had no political connections) that could have had an adverse effect on his career. So, he handled me with kid gloves but began to bob and weave, telling me that it wouldn't be possible to schedule a meeting with the president. Most of his reasoning was very sound and centered around "not enough time." I continued like I didn't even hear him. Finally, in a quasi-sarcastic tone, he said, "Mr. Lowry, do you have any idea how many people want to meet with the President of the United States?" I saw this as an opening and said, "Well, that's probably true, but you can count on one finger how many men just spent $20,000 running full-page, full-color ads—*supportive* ads of the president in the three largest newspapers in Florida, a state that is going to be critical to the president in the upcoming election." After a somewhat long pause, the man replied, in a now genteel tone, "Mr. Lowry, I'm going to have to get back to you tomorrow." "Great," I said, "I look forward to your call."

I was in my zone and totally focused on pulling off this meeting for Mr. Abraham. The next morning, I got a call back from Washington, D.C. The same gentleman I had spoken to a day earlier instructed me to contact Keech LeGrand. Keech headed up the advance team already in the area preparing for the president's visit. This was about the time that I got word that even if I could pull off a meeting with the president, Mr. Abraham (the honorary consul of Lebanon for thirty years) had obligations outside the country. Well, the way I looked at it, Tommy, Mr. Abraham's son who was running the dealership, would make a great surrogate. When I contacted Keech LeGrand, she was expecting my call. After explaining what we wanted to do, she was still having a hard time connecting the dots, so she suggested I come by their hotel headquarters for a personal meeting.

That afternoon I went to the hotel and when I walked in the place was buzzing. It looked like they had three adjoining rooms with about ten to twelve people working the phones. (At the time I remember being very impressed with all that was taking place. I had always been very interested in politics, and this bird's-eye view behind the scenes was a real treat!) When I finally got someone's attention, they directed me to a desk where Keech was talking with someone on the phone. After the call ended, I introduced myself and went on to again explain why I wanted to set up a meeting with the president and Tom Abraham. I brought a copy of the full-page article and said that I was going to have the article mounted with a little brass plaque commemorating the event. It was obvious that she had done her homework and knew exactly who Anthony Abraham was but still wasn't sure whether we'd get our meeting. She said she had to check with one other person and would call me back in the morning. To this day I can only speculate, but at the time I thought the "one other person" was either Chief of Staff Hamilton Jordan or the president himself.

Now for a little *schmooze* (this actually proved to be significant the following day)…

I left the hotel and drove to an iconic Tampa tradition, Alessi Bakery. I purchased two large cheesecakes and had them sent to Keech and her team at the hotel. Along with the cheesecakes was a note that said:

> Keech,
>
> It was nice meeting you today and whether you can arrange a meeting or not, I wanted to thank you for your efforts.
>
> Have a great day,
>
> Cody

The next morning, I had just finished giving a sales meeting and was headed to my office when I heard over the loudspeaker that I had a call from the White House. At the time, my calls were screened, but it was still odd to me that the receptionist used the words "White House," so I assumed it was a prank call from one of my fellow employees. I picked up the phone and it was Keech. She said she had some good news—they had arranged for a meeting with Tom Abraham and the president! Wow. I asked, "Would there be a chance that I could accompany Mr. Abraham?"

I guess at the time, although I had never formerly asked if I could tag along for the meeting, I had just assumed I would. Keech politely replied that that would not be possible. She went on to explain some preliminary things that needed to be taken care of, mostly related to security checks. When she finished with the details of the meeting, I gave it the old college try and once again asked if there wasn't any way I could accompany Mr. Abraham. I remember there being a somewhat long pause and then she responded, "Cody, I will handle it. Thanks for the cheesecake!"

When you look at the presidential daily diary for Jimmy Carter, it shows that on August 30, 1979, at 7:30 p.m., Thomas Abraham and Cody Lowry met with the president and presented him with a plaque of recognition. Today when I look at that diary, it becomes apparent that my request was perhaps a more daunting challenge than I thought it was at the time. Every detail and every minute of the president's schedule was accounted for. So, trying to squeeze in a meeting at the last moment was perhaps a very unrealistic and unorthodox request. Thanks again, Keech!

Not too long after the Carter meeting, I left the automotive retail business and opened an advertising agency in Tampa. In the early days of the agency, I had the opportunity to engage with an American self-made mogul, Mortimer Levitt. Mortimer Levitt built a men's fashion empire selling custom shirts. Mr. Levitt opened his first location in New York City and eventually had sixty stores in high-profile locations throughout the United States. The son of struggling immigrant parents, Mortimer Levitt authored five books and was a strong supporter of the arts, culture, and education. Today, the Levitt Foundation includes funding for ten permanent Levitt venues for the arts around the country.

Let me be frank—the day I called Mr. Levitt I had no idea how big this guy was. About ten weeks prior to my call I happened to walk into one of his stores in Fort Lauderdale (the Custom Shop).

When I walked in, I was greeted by a salesman who really knew what he was doing. When I told him that I was going to my first big convention in Dallas in a couple of months, that's all it took. One hour later, I was done. I had picked out three fabrics, my shirt measurements were taken, and I was given the promise that I would have my custom shirts delivered in about eight to ten weeks.

Wow—I couldn't believe it. My first custom shirts, and they were defiantly custom—high collar button-downs with pocket and French cuffs (something I wouldn't order today). I know this sounds a little shallow, but I thought of those custom shirts and their arrival almost every day. I think on the eighth week I started pestering my wife, Phyllis, "Hey, did my shirts come in?" Every night, and in a very loud voice, that was my loving greeting when I walked through the door. "Honey, I'm home. Did my shirts come in today?" With three kids all under the age of four, she had a lot more important things to worry about than His Majesty's Custom Shirts.

It was Saturday morning and the convention was about ten days away. I was starting to drive myself crazy with the thought of going to Dallas without my custom shirts. Sitting in the kitchen with my order numbers, I decided to call the Fort Lauderdale location to get some clarity as to the specific time my shirts would arrive. I got a very nice gentleman on the phone and explained the situation. I had ordered my shirts nine weeks ago, and if I didn't have them to go to my first big convention in Dallas, I would probably have to kill myself (that's not really what I said, but because my emotions were running high at the time he got the point...I wanted my shirts!!).

This man was very patient, and when I was done with my frantic plea he explained in a very monotonous delivery, almost like he had given the same explanation many times before, that because we were past the eight-week period, if he were to try and pull my order numbers at that point my shirts might get delayed by weeks. I didn't say anything. I just sat there quietly for a moment, trying to connect the dots. And then the gentlemen said, "Mr. Lowry, are you there?" "Yes, I'm still here," still thinking about what my next move might be. "Let me ask you a question," I said. "Who owns the Custom Shop?"

"Who owns the Custom Shop?" he repeated in the form of a question.

"Yes," I said.

His response was, "Well, he doesn't live in Fort Lauderdale."

At first, I thought that was a strange answer, but on further reflection that may have been the first time anyone had asked for the owner's name. "Well, that's fine," I said, "but who is the owner?"

"Well, his name is Mortimer Levitt."

"Would you possibly have a telephone number for him?"

The reply was quick and to the point, "No!"

We exchanged pleasantries and hung up. Because I knew the company was based out of New York, and because it was a Saturday, I called New York City information for the telephone number for Mortimer Levitt. What were the chances that he would have a listed number? Pretty good, apparently.

The operator gave me Mr. Levitt's home phone number. I will never forget what happened next, and it always brings a smile to my face. I started dialing the number, when Phyllis blurted out (holding both hands over her ears), "What are you doing??" That was a very easy question for me to answer. "I'm calling Mortimer… maybe he can help me get my shirts." I finished dialing and the phone started to ring. A lady answered (Mrs. Levitt, I presumed). "Hello. Is Mortimer Levitt available?"

"Who's calling?" she said.

"This is Cody Lowry from Florida."

Mrs. Levitt then screamed out, "Mort, it's about the property in Florida."

Mr. Levitt got on the phone, and he couldn't have been nicer, even when I told him the call was not about property in Florida, but about my shirts. He listened to my whole story, and I'm sure he was terribly impressed with my big trip to Dallas. Then he lowered the boom. "Cody, let me tell you why that's not going to be possible." He then went on to parrot the gentleman in Fort Lauderdale... because the order was past eight weeks, if they were to pull those orders now the shirts could be delayed weeks.

At this point, I started *schmoozing* and groveling at the same time. I told him about the great service I had gotten at his Lauderdale location (which was true). "Mr. Levitt, I have a company and I know that at times I have to do things out of the ordinary to accommodate a customer. Isn't there anything you can do to make sure I get my shirts?"

"OK," he said, "this is what I'm going to do. Give me the order numbers. I can't promise you anything but let me see what I can do." That was Saturday morning. Tuesday afternoon the shirts were delivered to my house in Lakeland, Florida.

I didn't know it at the time, but Mr. Levitt and I may have had some things in common. Mimi Levitt, Mortimer's wife, once said of her late husband, "He was quite a character, a real original. He never cared what other people did. He did things his way."

Many times, we are faced with situations where we follow the crowd instead of being the contrarian. When somebody says it's not possible, or that it can't be done, refer to one of my favorite poems since college.

It Couldn't Be Done

Somebody said that it couldn't be done
But he with a chuckle replied
That "maybe it couldn't," but he would be one
Who wouldn't say so till he'd tried.
So he buckled right in with the trace of a grin
On his face. If he worried he hid it.
He started to sing as he tackled the thing
That couldn't be done, and he did it!
Somebody scoffed: "Oh, you'll never do that;
At least no one ever has done it,"
But he took off his coat and he took off his hat
And the first thing we knew he'd begun it.
With a lift of his chin and a bit of a grin,
Without any doubting or quiddit,
He started to sing as he tackled the thing
That couldn't be done, and he did it.
There are thousands to tell you it cannot be done,
There are thousands to prophesy failure,
There are thousands to point out to you one by one,
The dangers that wait to assail you.
But just buckle in with a bit of a grin,
Just take off your coat and go to it;
Just start in to sing as you tackle the thing
That "cannot be done," and you'll do it.

— EDGAR ALBERT GUEST

The Takeaway

If we live our lives according to Hoyle and always play by established rules, we run the risk of falling short of our full potential. Maybe it's time to reboot and consider tapping into your contrarian gene pool and start swimming against the current. The important thing to remember is that we can't hit it out of the park if we're not willing to step up to the plate. By trusting in yourself and paying attention to your own gut feeling, you'll give yourself some surprising victories that you'll remember for a lifetime.

Chapter Five

CALL ME CRAZY

"To Sparky with blessings."

—POPE JOHN PAUL II

What exactly does "thinking big" mean to you? For me, it's about looking at something that seems improbable on the surface, then forging ahead and formulating a plan to make it happen. English billionaire, investor, and philanthropist Sir Richard Branson once said: "If people aren't calling you crazy, you aren't thinking big enough."

Before I share an incredible story about thinking big (and yes, many called it a crazy idea), I want to introduce you to my accomplice who shared equal billing in the execution and success of this wild idea: the High Priest of *Schmooze*, Monsignor John P. Caulfield.

In the 1944 movie *Going My Way*, Bing Crosby portrayed an American Irish priest named Father Charles O'Malley. In the movie, Father O'Malley was sent to take over a rough and rundown Midtown Manhattan parish. He was portrayed as a kind, spiritual, and empathetic young priest who had everyone's interest at heart. Father Caulfield also had all those attributes, but so much more. For the twenty-five years we spent together, I can tell you that he was a rock star in Lakeland, Florida—a rock star who shared his Irish charm, wit, intellect, and compassion with everyone who crossed his path.

Bing Crosby went on to win the Academy Award for Best Actor for that film. *Going My Way* also won six additional awards including Best Picture. If they gave Academy Awards for how one fulfills their life's work here on Earth, Father Caulfield's awards would fill to capacity the world's largest trophy case. He would also win the Lifetime Achievement Award for giving 100 percent of his life and every waking hour to the physical and spiritual needs of all those he encountered.

Several years ago, someone in our community remarked in a casual conversation that I was Father Caulfield's best friend. I quickly corrected him because nothing could have been further from the truth. Father didn't have just one best friend, because we were all his best friend, and he genuinely cared for all of us. If he did have a best friend, it was whoever he was with at the moment. That person knew that was *their* time and that they had Father's undivided attention. If you could talk to the many people (of all faiths) who knew and worked with Father Caulfield during his twenty-seven years serving the Lakeland community, you'd come away with some wonderful and incredible stories. Here's mine…

John was born in the village of Claregalway in County Galway, Ireland. He was the oldest brother to seven siblings: Teresa, Eamonn, Eileen, Mary, Joe, Patrick, and Matt. It was customary at the time for the oldest son to take over the family farm, but John (to the great fortune of those he touched in life) chose to become a priest instead. He graduated from St. Peter's College in Wexford, Ireland, and was ordained in May of 1959. His first assignment was for the Diocese of St. Augustine, which served most of Florida at that time. In 1962, he furthered his education and earned a master of arts in both Greek and Latin from Catholic University of America in Washington, D.C. For the next ten years, Father Caulfield worked in several churches and schools throughout central Florida and in 1972 was appointed to Our Lady of Lourdes Parish in Melbourne, Florida. This is where the genesis of our relationship took place.

Coincidentally, Father's longtime secretary at Our Lady of Lourdes was Peggy Davis, the sister of Dick Davis (highlighted in chapter three). I would occasionally see Peggy at Davis family get-togethers. Peggy was a wonderful lady and, while I didn't know her well at the time, I learned years later that she knew me very well. Mainly, she knew of the struggle I had during my formative years, so when Father Caulfield was transferred in 1984 to St. Joseph's Parish in Lakeland, and I made Lakeland my new home as well, Peggy was dead set on getting us together. She would say in many conversations over the years that this was a convergence made in Heaven, and that I needed to take care of Father and Father needed to take care of me.

It was during this time that I was under strict instructions from Peggy to reach out to Father Caulfield and that he'd be expecting my call. This set-up would become a very funny first meeting (I'm actually laughing now just thinking of this inaugural conclave!). I called Father early one week and hadn't gotten a call back, so I called a second time. His secretary informed me that Father was looking forward to our meeting, that he'd be returning to his office in about thirty minutes, and that she would make sure to have him call. Because I only lived six blocks from the school and church, I decided to head over to his office and meet the good Padre in person.

As fate would have it, no sooner had I pulled into a parking space when Father pulled into one two spaces down, with an empty space between us. The Father had never laid eyes on me, so he had no idea what I looked like. I, on the other hand, knew this was definitely Father Caulfield—not only did he have on his collar, but this guy looked like he had just come out of central casting with the starring role of Father Flanagan in *Boys Town*. You should know that back then (and to this day), it wasn't unusual for me to inject a little humor when meeting someone for the first time, so I thought I'd have a little fun when Father got out of his car. I decided to startle him with a very unfriendly greeting. In an aggressive, combative tone that would give anyone the impression that I was looking for a fight, I screamed out, "Excuse me, are you Father Caulfield?" He turned around with a look on his face to let me know that if I were looking for a fight, he'd be happy to accommodate. Then, in his distinct Irish brogue, he responded in a tone equally as aggressive as mine, "I am indeed!" Now, let's be clear, Father would have been about fifty-two at the time and in incredible shape. He would've been able to squash me like a mosquito. Having played soccer and hurling back in Ireland, he was very athletic and played racket or handball at least twice a week with his good friend Father Peter Quinn, who pastored at the neighboring parish of St. Anthony's. Father Caulfield was built like a lumberjack! His hands were massive, and if he ever made a fist, it looked as big (if not bigger) than the size of the fists of most heavyweight boxers.

I'm sure no one had addressed him like that since his school-yard days as a teenager back home in Ireland. So, when I fired back in the same aggressive tone, "Well, is there any particular reason why you haven't returned my call?" Father had fire in his eyes! Before he could respond (and while I was still on my feet!), I started laughing and said, "It's me, Father…Cody Lowry." He then started laughing and responded as he did for the next twenty-five years whenever I was trying to get his goat—in a very long and drawn out pronunciation of my last name that could be heard by anyone within fifty feet. He said, "*L-o-w-r-y!*"

Over the next twenty-five years, he'd let out a roaring "*L-o-w-r-y*" too many times to recall. One incident that stands out in my mind is the time we were on the golf course. We walked to the tee box and introduced ourselves to two gentlemen with whom we'd be playing that day. After the introduction, I said in a concerned voice that could easily be heard by our playing partners, "Be careful, Father...they're Protestants." With eyes wide-open, Father responded, "*L-o-w-r-y!*"

We became fast friends and, because I lived right down the street, he'd often seek refuge at our home (as well as other homes, including longtime friends Kevin and Maureen Brown) to just sit and relax after a long twelve- or fourteen-hour day. Until he retired at the age of seventy-six, Father kept this incredible pace. He would start most weekdays giving the 6 a.m. mass, and then his daily grind would take him in any number of directions: business meetings for the school and church, visiting people in the hospital, visiting parishioners who were homebound, and so on. One of his favorite weekly destinations was one of Florida's state prisons. Jokingly, he would say the reason he loved his prison ministry so much was because he had a *captive* audience.

Father Caulfield, the High Priest of *Schmooze*, with his keen intellect, his sense of humor, and that winning smile, always had the right response for any situation that may have come up. When my wife, Phyllis, and I got married, we were not married in the Catholic Church. I was Catholic, but Phyllis was not, and the church would not recognize her first marriage. If we wanted to get married in the church, Phyllis would've had to have gotten that marriage annulled. Well, that was out of the question for several reasons, not the least of which was the fact that with my marriage to Phyllis came a very special gift, my beautiful stepdaughter and first child, Marni. Having Phyllis's first marriage annulled would've put Marni's legitimacy into question, and that was just not going to happen.

Father pursued many avenues with the Diocese of Orlando to no avail, including Phyllis going through a nine-month program called RCIA (Right of Christian Initiation of Adults) to convert to the Catholic Church. Finally, Father decided that he'd take matters into his own hands. While I was out of town one day, he called Phyllis to arrange a time for us to be married in the church. It was a very low-key ceremony in the chapel adjacent to the big church with just Phyllis and me, the kids, and a few friends.

Now for some Irish *schmooze*...

Father started the ceremony, but suddenly stopped dead in his tracks. He looked me right in the eye and in a deep Irish brogue said, "Cody, I need to see you in the sacristy." I had no idea what was going on, but since this was his show, up the steps we both went to the sacristy. Father seemed a bit serious and that made me a little nervous. Then out it came, "Cody, I need to take your confession." Did he just say "confession"? Confession...as in tell the good Father all the sins I had committed over the last seven years. Really?? We weren't even in an enclosed confessional. While I wanted to say, "Father, I know this sounds unusual, but I can't remember my last sin," I sat there in dead silence looking back at him like I had just seen a ghost. Finally, Father came to my rescue saying, "Don't worry, Cody, I'll do the talking."

One of Father's great talents was conducting funerals. He was a master. Never canned, his funerals were poignant, sincere, on target, and always laced with just the right dose of humor. Whenever I asked how a funeral went, he would reply in that Irish brogue, "Cody, we gave him a good send-off." I had always hoped that when the time came, he would be there to give me a good send-off. Unfortunately, it didn't work out that way. When his time came, the city of Lakeland and the parishioners of St. Joseph's Church—his flock that he loved so much—gave Monsignor Caulfield one incredible send-off. Attendance was a thousand strong, including sixty priests, with Bishop John Noonan from the Diocese of Orlando officiating the funeral. I was honored to speak along with his brother Joe, who had made the trip from his home in Scotland, and parishioner and dear friend of Monsignor, Kevin Browne.

I have attended many funerals, and as the tears begin to well up as I write about that day, I will never forget watching the number of grown men who under the most extreme circumstances would keep a stiff upper lip, openly sobbing as they said their farewell to their friend and their priest. As I walked out of the church, I remember feeling totally drained. I had spent the last three weeks at Father's side in the hospital, along with an incredible lady and nurse. One of us was always at his side monitoring any needs, as well as trying to manage the constant flow of people who wanted to visit him in the hospital. Father's body was to be sent back to his home in Galway, where there would be another service and burial. As I was making my way to Monsignor's reception, one of his relatives from Ireland ran up to me. "Cody, you must go to Ireland and tell Father's story." I respectfully explained that it wouldn't be possible and that I had pretty much neglected my business for almost a month. Well, that was that…or so I thought.

At the reception, the same gentleman, along with a reinforcement of additional family members, encouraged me to reconsider, emphasizing once again the importance of having me deliver Father's story across the pond. As reluctant as I was, I was no match for this group's enthusiasm and collective purpose. Two days later, Bishop Noonan, Father's two brothers (Joe and Matt), and I were off to Ireland, where I had the honor to deliver a narrative on the life of a man I so greatly admired.

St Joseph's School in Lakeland, Florida, is a Catholic parochial school. A parochial school is different from a private school in that, at a private Catholic school, expenses are primarily paid through tuitions, as opposed to a parochial Catholic school, where the school is part of a larger community, tuitions are lower, and the expenses are usually financially supported by the parish and church. At a parochial school, there's a lot of pressure on the parents to continually find ways to generate funds to keep tuitions low and keep the school on a financially even keel. For almost twenty years, I was a member of St. Joseph's Educational Foundation, which Father Caulfield, along with some wonderful St. Joseph's parishioners (who over the years I have fondly referred to as visionaries) established in 1991. I was elected to the board in 1992, and as the young pup I came loaded with new ways to raise money for the foundation.

One idea I suggested to my fellow board members, and I will admit it was not terribly novel even at that time, was an annual golf tournament. The big push-back from board members, as well as some parents, was that there were already too many golf tournaments in town, and that we would end up spending a lot of time, money, and effort with very little upside. I'm a pretty good listener and I'm not averse to heeding the advice of others; however, even though I thought their arguments were sound, Father and I decided that a golf tournament would be a good idea for the foundation, even if we didn't make a dime. Our rationale was simple—even if the tournament was not a financial success, we would bring some much-needed awareness to the new school foundation.

My first challenge was to make sure that we held the tournament at a venue that was special. *Special* in that I wanted it to be a course where I knew our target group had never played. So, instead of having our tournament at one of several public (and much cheaper) courses in the area, I reached out to a private club in Lakeland called the Lone Palm Golf Club. Publix Super Market's home base is in Lakeland, and Lone Palm has been owned and operated by the Publix Corporation for decades.

The club was built by Publix founder George Jenkins in 1964, and to this day it is still a coveted place for non-members to play. With this great inaugural venue in place, I ran an idea by Father, and he loved it. We both agreed that a high-profile honorary chairman would be just the right touch to lend a little cachet to our very first tournament. Well, no pun intended when I tell you that we knocked it out of the park! Our choice was Sparky Anderson, manager of the Detroit Tigers, who spent spring training in Lakeland. Since our tournament was scheduled in late February, the timing was perfect. And because Sparky was a devout Catholic who attended daily mass at St Joseph's, he was no stranger to Father and the downtown Catholic community.

When Father told Sparky what we had in mind, he graciously agreed to be our chairman, and thanks to Sparky and our incredible volunteers from both the school and the parish, our first tournament was an overwhelming success. In little Lakeland, Florida—a town with a population of less than 100,000 at the time, and a town that purportedly had too many golf tournaments—we had to stop taking players at 140 and we raised over $50,000 that first year for the St. Joseph's Educational Foundation.

After two years, Sparky decided that it would be a good idea for him to step down and for us to reach out to someone other than himself to be the tournament's honorary chairman. Finding a replacement was just as easy as finding our first. I asked a dear friend of mine, Super Bowl-winning coach and now member of the prestigious NFL Hall of Fame, Hank Stram. He accepted with no reservations.

One morning while having breakfast with Father, we discussed doing something nice for Sparky for all he had done to put our tournament on the map in the Lakeland community. Father's first suggestion was a nice piece of Waterford Crystal, and while Sparky would have been delighted, I just thought we should be a little more creative (and, yes, *think outside the box*). Being the honorary chairman didn't only mean lending your name to the tournament, it also meant playing in the tournament and speaking at the dinner and auction after the tournament. Sparky was so gracious and was affectionately approached by the hundreds of players, volunteers, and club personnel seeking an autograph or just wanting to say a few words to one of baseball's legends. I felt that that kind of commitment deserved a special effort, so I just blurted out, "Father, why don't we get Sparky a baseball autographed by the pope?" To which he replied laughing with his Irish accent, "*L-o-w-r-y.*" (I can see him laughing like it was yesterday.) I returned the laughter with a stoic look that let him know I was serious and ready to charge.

When breakfast ended, I had convinced the High Priest of *Schmooze* that, as crazy as it sounded, it was worth a try. Two days later, I sent the Vatican a MLB baseball and a black Paper Mate pen for signing. Along with the ball and pen was a letter that gave the reason for my request. I explained who Sparky was and how he'd helped us raise almost $100,000 for St. Joseph's Educational Foundation in just over two years. Well, I waited almost two weeks and finally received a package from the Vatican. I almost couldn't wait to open the box! And when I did, there was my unsigned baseball along with the Paper Mate. There was also a return letter that gave the reasons why the pope (Pope John Paul II) was not able to sign the ball. In short, the pope doesn't do baseballs!

I knew it was time for a second pitch, but I didn't really have any other avenues to pursue. And then—call it divine intervention—I received a call from Father Caulfield telling me that our bishop of the Dioceses of Orlando, Bishop Norbert M. Dorsey, was off to the Vatican, where he was going to have an audience with the pope, and that he would try and get the ball signed. When Bishop Dorsey gave the reasons why, the pope asked, "What does *Sparky* mean?" The bishop explained that Sparky was a nickname given to him for his fiery personality. The pope acquiesced and signed the ball to Sparky! In Latin he wrote, "To Sparky with blessings."

About a week later, Bishop Dorsey was back in Florida and called Father to let him know that he was successful in getting Pope John Paul II to sign Sparky's ball. When Father called to let me know, the only person more ecstatic than me was Father himself. He already had it figured out. We'd invite Sparky to dinner and present him with the ball. While that sounded like a good idea, I knew this deserved something bigger than dinner for three. I suggested to Father that we needed to think this through. This was *big* on several fronts...for Sparky, the city of Lakeland, and to create awareness for our newly formed St. Joseph's Educational Foundation.

For over 125 years, Major League Baseball has migrated to Florida during February and March to prepare for upcoming baseball seasons with spring training. During the latter part of February and the month of March, Florida is rich with many big-time baseball players, as well as legends of the game. It was for that reason that we chose this time to surprise and present this very special ball to Sparky. Instead of three of us getting together for dinner, we decided on three hundred. On February 23, 1994, the St. Joseph Educational Foundation held a charity gala celebration for Sparky, that coincidentally was also Sparky's sixtieth birthday week (Sparky Anderson: February 22, 1934–November 4, 2010). We didn't have a venue big enough at St. Joseph, so we decided to have the event at the Santa Fe Catholic High School gymnasium. Now, I know a gymnasium doesn't sound terribly glamorous for a gala of any kind, but when our volunteers got through decorating, the ambience rivaled something you might expect at the Waldorf Astoria. There was only one missing piece to our well-planned evening— who could we reach out to that could really *knock it out of the park*? Once again, we had to think *big*.

In 1994, the Los Angeles Dodgers' spring training was at Holman Stadium in Vero Beach, about a two-hour drive from

Lakeland. Their manager was none other than one of the all-time greats and best personalities of the game, then and now, Tommy Lasorda. Tommy spent sixty-eight seasons with the Brooklyn/L.A. Dodgers in one capacity or another, edging out Dodger broadcaster Vin Scully as the longest serving Dodger by two seasons. For our tribute to Sparky, we didn't even have a back-up plan because the perennial favorite on everyone's list was the great Tommy Lasorda. When we reached out and asked if he would be our master of ceremonies and to help us surprise Sparky, he graciously and quickly agreed. Tommy was, as you might expect, great that evening. From the time I introduced him to the audience (that included many current Detroit Tiger players, as well as past greats like "Mr. Tiger" himself, Al Kaline), Tommy was the perfect touch.

When it came time for the grand finale, the surprise presentation to Sparky of a baseball signed by Pope John Paul II, our audience was on the edge of their seats. The overwhelming majority of the St. Joseph crowd knew what the surprise was, and they couldn't wait. Tommy Lasorda invited me, along with Father Caulfield and Bishop Dorsey, to the stage. When we invited Sparky, a devout Catholic, to come forward and we presented him with the ball, he was clearly in shock. This wonderful person, who in my presence never turned down anyone who wanted an autograph, definitely had the tables turned on him (or in today's vernacular, Sparky got punked)! He really was in a state of shock and when he did address the audience, he let everyone know that this was an evening he would never forget, and that the ball was the cherished gift of a lifetime. Today, that baseball signed by Pope John Paul II sits in the Baseball Hall of Fame in Cooperstown, New York. Sparky later said, kiddingly, "I didn't want it in my house because if my kids got down and out, they might take it to the memorabilia shop." It was indeed a great evening, giving some much-needed awareness to our new foundation (not to mention the several thousand dollars we raised that night). The gala actually made national news. *USA Today* did a story, as did the *Detroit Free Press* and *The* (Lakeland) *Ledger*.

We all have great ideas, but if we don't act on them, or if we don't follow through, they quickly become just ideas, and then eventually they become just lost memories in our minds. If we sit back and over-rationalize or overthink our big ideas, we run the risk of convincing ourselves of all the reasons why they won't succeed. Perhaps the great Winston Churchill said it best: "No idea is so outlandish that it should not be considered with a searching, but at the same time a steady eye."

Gijs van Wulfen, author and global speaker on innovation, in his article "10 Great Ideas That Were Originally Rejected," writes that "history has shown us that a lot of wise people haven't been able to recognize the potential of a great idea."

1) "This 'telephone' has too many shortcomings to be seriously considered as a means of communication. The device is inherently of no value to us."—Western Union internal memo dated 1876.

2) "I do not believe the introduction of motor-cars will ever affect the riding of horses."—Mr. John Doug-las-Scott-Montagu, MP, United Kingdom, 1903.

3) "The wireless music box has no imaginable commercial value. Who would pay for a message sent to nobody in particular?"—David Sarnoff's associates rejecting a proposal for investment in the radio in the 1920s.

4) "Who the hell wants to hear actors talk?"—H.M. Warner (Warner Brothers) before rejecting a proposal for movies with sound in 1927.

5) "This is typical Berlin hot air. The product is worthless."—Heinrich Dreser, head of Bayer's Pharmacological Institute, rejecting Felix Hoffman's invention of aspirin.

6) "Who the hell wants to copy a document on plain paper???!!!!"—Rejection letter, in 1940, to Chester Carlson, inventor of the Xerox machine.

7) "The concept is interesting and well-formed, but in order to earn better than a 'C', the idea must be feasible."—Yale university professor in response to Fred Smith's paper proposing reliable overnight delivery service. Smith went on to found Federal Express.

8) "There is no reason anyone would want a computer in their home."—Ken Olsen, president, chairman, and founder of Digital Equipment Corporation, in 1977.

9) "You want to have consistent and uniform muscle development across all of your muscles? It can't be done. It's just a fact of life. You just have to accept inconsistent muscle development as an unalterable condition of weight training."—Rejection letter to Arthur Jones, inventor of the Nautilus fitness machine.

10) "So, we went to Atari and said, 'Hey, we've got this amazing thing, even built with some of your parts, and what do you think about funding us? Or we'll give it to you. We just want to do it. Pay our salary, we'll come work for you.' And they said, 'No.' So then we went to Hewlett-Packard and they said, 'Hey, we don't need you. You haven't got through college yet.'"—Steve Jobs on attempts to get Atari and HP interested in his and Steve Wozniak's personal computer.

There are many reasons we don't follow through with our ideas. Perhaps the biggest is that we don't set up concrete execution plans to turn our ideas into realities. When I decided that I was going to write this book and then started writing it, I had an execution plan that would help keep me on track. I think my number one tactic was not only sharing my idea for the book to family and friends but also sending them a "mock-up" of the book cover, along with the first chapter.

It wasn't long before I had built an enthusiastic cheerleading squad. Hardly a week went by when someone didn't ask me how the book was coming along. That alone was a big help for me in overcoming one of my biggest faults—procrastination, something that has plagued me my whole life (that reminds me, I promised my wife I would take out the garbage hours ago). I'm not sure who said this, but no truer words on the subject of ideas have ever been written: "Good ideas are written on paper. Great ideas are put into motion."

The Takeaway

I was only ten years old when David J. Schwartz wrote *The Magic of Thinking Big*. Today, over six million copies have sold, and for good reason. The information in that book is as relevant today as it was sixty years ago. Here's a rundown of five life lessons that we can learn today from this iconic book:

1. Believe you can succeed, and you will.

2. Stop making excuses.

3. Build confidence and destroy fear.

4. Think and dream creatively.

5. You are what you think you are.

When it's your time to shine…when it's your moment…when you run the risk of people calling you crazy—that's great! Forget about being practical. Author and speaker, Simon Sinek, nailed it when he said, "We should never let reality interfere with our dreams. Reality can't see what we can see."

Chapter Six

SCHMOOZING
ON THE LINKS

"Of all the hazards, fear is the worst."

— SAM SNEAD

Golf is and has been a very big part of my life. With that said, I've never had, nor will I ever have, a game that matches my passion. Perhaps my game was best described by Kevin Walker, the head golf pro at the Nantucket Club. I was invited to play this prestigious course with my good friend Johnny Ricotta, who lives in Chatham, Cape Cod. After a nice, leisurely round with Kevin Walker and caddies, Kevin evaluated everybody's round. He went down the line and gave a quick small tip to everyone to help them better their game. I was last, and when he got to me, he paused, and with a great big smile said, "Cody, you do everything right…you just don't do them in the right order."

We all had a good laugh because it was funny, and for the most part, I knew it was true. I got both of my boys, Cody Jr. and Kipp, playing at an early age, and today I'm proud of their low single-digit handicaps. Whenever I'm fortunate to play with one of the boys and they hit one of those 300-yard drives right down the middle, I can often be heard bragging for everyone to hear, "Apples don't fall far from the tree." It always gets a big laugh because it's so far from reality. I always tell people that my boys started playing at eight and I started playing at thirty-eight.

I have been fortunate, though, because in addition to playing some fabulous venues in the States as well as other parts of the world, I've played some of the most prestigious and hard-to-get-on courses anywhere. Three years ago, I had the opportunity, along with my good friends Damien Lamendola and Joe Kedzuf, to play the Muirfield Golf Club in Gullane, Scotland. Muirfield is one of the courses used in rotation for the Open Championship and is best known for producing the first "Rules of Golf" back in 1744. Getting on can be extremely difficult. That day, however, we were very lucky. We played eighteen holes in the morning, then showered, and put on coats and ties, and had lunch in the men's dining room, followed by another eighteen holes in the afternoon. On this trip to Scotland we played eleven rounds in eight days:

1. The Old Course
2. The New Course
3. Kings Barn 2
4. Carnoustie
5. Muirfield 2
6. North Berwick
7. Trump Aberdeen 2
8. Cruden Bay

St. Andrews (the Old Course) is an absolute must for any golf enthusiast heading across the pond. I mention St. Andrews not because it's hard to get on, but because it isn't. It's open to the public, and if you don't have a set time prearranged with one of the private tour companies, you'll have to be part of their daily lottery. If and when you're picked, they assign a tee time for your group. I recommend the Old Course for one reason and one reason alone—it is considered (by most) the "home of golf." Established in 1552, it is the oldest and most iconic course in the world. When you're standing on that first tee with the Royal and Ancient Clubhouse at your back, you get the sense that you are truly standing on hallowed ground. It was on the Old Course at St. Andrews that one of the world's greatest golfers of all time, Arnold Palmer, summed it up as well as anyone: "This is the origin of the game, golf in its purest form, and it's still played that way on a course seemingly untouched by time. Every time I play here, it reminds me that this is still a game."

Over the years, I've been invited to play some very private golf courses, including the Bel Air Country Club in Los Angeles, where the likes of Jack Nicholson, Kelsey Grammar, Clint Eastwood, and Tom Cruise are members. The late business mogul and famed recluse Howard Hughes was also a member and was known for landing his plane on the course because he was late for a date with Katherine Hepburn.

I've also teed it up at Medina with my good friend Jon Anderson, as well as Butler National, both located in the Chicago area. I've also had the good fortune of playing the iconic and world-renowned Pine Valley Golf Club in New Jersey three times and have been able to host clients because of a very special friend who is also a member, golf architect Steve Smyers. Past president of the American Society of Golf Course Architects and past treasurer of the USGA Executive Committee, Steve is a guy who could have written this book. A true class act with an engaging personality, Steve was a member of the 1973 University of Florida golf team that included Andy Bean, Gary Koch, and Andy North, as well as Fred Ridley, who today is chairman of Augusta National Golf Club. Because of Steve, I have been fortunate to *schmooze* and entertain some important clients and friends (including sons Cody and Kipp, and son-in-law Noel Taylor). All the money in the world won't get you on at Pine Valley unless you are with a playing member.

For those of you non-golfers, Pine Valley is one of the more extreme challenges in the game of golf. The late comedian Bob Hope, who shot a first-round 103 with a ten on a par three, remarked, "Foursomes have left the first tee and have never been seen again." Pine Valley is consistently ranked the number-one or number-two course in America, and some would rank it number one in the world. The member list reads like an international *Who's Who* of business, finance, industry, and entertainment, with a large contingency of PGA and European players, and the board of directors are the only ones allowed to extend an invitation to join this elite club.

Now, I know some of you are probably wondering at this point, "But what about the Big Daddy…one of the most iconic and prestigious golf courses in the world, Augusta National Golf Club, where golf's most popular tournament (the Masters) is played each year?" OK, here's what happened…

The idiom "birds of a feather" (meaning people having similar characteristics, backgrounds, interests, and beliefs) certainly applies in my life, especially when it comes to having that *schmooze* personality. As you read this book, many of you are reflecting and identifying with people in your own life—family members, friends, co-workers, bosses—who carry the *schmooze* gene. For me, this book would not be complete without including my brother-in-*schmooze*, Steve Mauldin. Steve has spent his life in the television industry and today is president of the CBS-owned station in Los Angeles. In 1998, Steve was General Manager of WTSP in St. Petersburg, Florida (a CBS affiliate), and I was running my own advertising agency in the Tampa Bay market. At the time, my agency represented the Chevrolet Local Market Association that consisted of twelve dealers throughout the Tampa Bay area. Steve had been in Tampa for about four years, and we had become pretty good friends. When I got a call from Steve one early February asking if I wanted to accompany him to the Masters in April of that year, it took all of two seconds to accept.

I was excited for many reasons, not the least of which was that I was going to the Masters as a guest of CBS, and I knew that would be special on many fronts. We would stay at a house CBS had rented in the town of Augusta. We'd have special credentials that would allow us to have access to almost any place on the course. I was also aware that Steve, having an advanced degree in *schmooze*, was very well liked by the head people at the CBS affiliate office in New York. Steve had us bring our golf clubs but was very upfront with the fact that, while we might get a round in, we couldn't count on playing Augusta. We arrived at our house Wednesday afternoon. It was a two-story in a nice neighborhood in what I would consider at the time the "upper end" for this small Southern town. When I went upstairs to my room, I was greeted with a large green swag bag, loaded with an assortment of Masters Tournament gear and souvenirs. There was also a letter on the bed addressed to me, welcoming me to Augusta, along with an invite for dinner that night.

Because of the nature of my business, I have attended many, many big (and sometimes over-the-top) dinners, but I have never experienced anything, then or now, like I experienced that evening. The venue was somewhat off the beaten path, and when Steve and I pulled up to the location, I remember thinking to myself, "This can't be it." In my opinion, the place was too small for what I was expecting, and there weren't that many cars in the parking lot. When Steve and I walked in, however, I was blown away. There were forty to fifty people in this very upscale room, several members of Augusta National, CBS station owners from around the country, and the entire CBS golf analyst team, including Jim Nantz and Ken Venturi. As part of the evening, every CBS analyst gave their take and handicap of what to expect that weekend. Well, I guess my initial expectations of the evening were right—it was over the top and a night that I will never forget.

The next morning a limousine picked Steve and me up to take us to play golf at a new course outside of Augusta. After driving for what seemed like a long time, it occurred to me that this guy might be lost and we for sure would be late for our assigned tee time. When we asked our driver if that was in fact the case, he answered in the affirmative. Remember, this was a new course and Google Maps was way off in the future. When we finally arrived, we were about fifteen minutes late. We drove up to the first tee, where our two playing partners were patiently waiting. We grabbed our clubs and shoes and headed to the tee box, where we were going to immediately start the round.

Now, I always play better if I have some time to warm up, but that was not to be the case on this day. As Steve and I were putting on our shoes in a rushed manner, I was introduced to the other two gentlemen. One of our playing partners, Les, teed off first. Les was left-handed and as he was going through his pre-swing drill, I thought I would break the ice with a little humor, since we really didn't get a chance to get acquainted. When Les was at the top of his very slow and deliberate left-handed golf swing, coming down to strike his drive, I screamed, "Les!" Before he could hit the ball, he abruptly stopped and looked at me, probably anticipating some sort of an emergency. Very calmly and with a stone-sober look on my face, I delivered one of the oldest one-liners in golf. "Les," I said, "you're standing on the wrong side of the ball." Everyone had a good laugh, including Les. And, yes, I felt it broke the ice and took the edge off (I know it did for me).

As we started the round, Steve put his clubs on the cart with Les, I put my clubs on with our other playing partner, and off we went. We hadn't gotten very far down the first fairway when this guy looked over at me and with a little smile on his face said, "You know most people don't screw with him." "Who...Les?" I said. He then went on to inform me that Les was the highest-paid executive with CBS and president of their entertainment division. For me, it will always be one of my most memorable rounds because it eventually was the catalyst for me playing one of the rounds of my life at Augusta National.

After we finished the match, we grabbed a drink in the clubhouse and Les asked if I was playing Monday, the day reserved for national sponsors. I told him no, and without commenting one way or the other, the subject was dropped. That evening when I went to my room, there was an envelope lying on my bed with my name on it. When I opened it, I almost couldn't believe it! In part, it read:

> YOU HAVE BEEN INVITED TO PLAY
> AUGUSTA NATIONAL.
>
> YOU WILL TEE OFF ON MONDAY, APRIL 13
> AT 9:30 AM.

Steve got the same invite. Even though he had played Augusta before, I could tell he was just as excited as I was. When we arrived at the cabin Monday morning, we were greeted by Les, who was going to play ahead of us with some national clients (including the chief marketing officer for Coca-Cola at the time, Sergio Zyman). You know, I have never been considered a "stick in the mud," but if I were, there's a good chance I wouldn't have played Augusta National. First, I wouldn't have been invited to the Masters tournament by Steve, and then there's no way CBS would have invited me to play Augusta National. What's interesting is that this magical round would never have happened had Mark O'Meara, who won his first major championship on that day in 1998, not made a twenty-foot birdie putt on the final hole to win the tournament. In 2004, the Masters went to a sudden death playoff where, if there is a tie, extra holes are played that day to determine a winner.

In 1998, however, players would have an eighteen-hole playoff on Monday. Monday, then, is the day special guests and sponsors have an opportunity to play the *grande dame* of golf, Augusta National. On the final hole of the tournament, I was snuggled up on eighteen with other fans, watching Mark O'Meara preparing his putt, when it suddenly occurred to me that if he didn't make this putt I was not going to play on Monday—that time would be reserved for a playoff round with Mark, Freddie Couples (who was on the green watching the putt himself), and David Duval (also tied for the lead). The oddsmakers in Las Vegas would've bet that, under this pressure and the incredible circumstances surrounding his first major win, Mark O'Meara would not make that putt. The golf gods were looking down on Mark that day, and I believe on me as well (albeit to a much lesser extent). When the putt went in for the win, the crowd, along with Mark, went wild, and I celebrated as well because I was going to tee it up at Augusta the following day.

Schmoozing on the links is something I have been doing with clients for years. It's an opportunity to build new relationships and to solidify relationships with current clients as well. Up until 2014, however, I can honestly say that I had never picked up an account during a round. That all changed one cool, sunny July morning, when I was paired up with my new client-to-be at Ballybunion Golf Club in Ballybunion, a costal seaside resort in County Kerry, Ireland. Ballybunion Golf Club was founded in 1893 and is considered one of the best links courses in the world. I was there on a client trip hosted by Cox Broadcasting. In the media and advertising world, it's common for media properties to entertain select clients as a way of thanking them for their business. These trips are awarded to their best clients or to accounts that have increased their spending over the prior year. In my case, I was invited for neither of those reasons. Call it the *schmooze factor*, but I was invited because one of their bigger clients arranged for me and my wife, Phyllis, to be invited. On this trip, our accommodations were spectacular—Adare Manor, a five-star castle resort located in County Limerick, a one-hour drive to the east of Ballybunion.*

Now, it would be considered taboo or rude for me to actively try and engage or encourage one of Cox Broadcasting's clients or other agencies' clients to do business with my company while on one of these trips. For that reason, I have always been extremely careful on any of these media trips to never give even the slightest impression that I was there for anything other than a little R&R. Local TV stations have on their client list advertisers who are considered "direct accounts." These accounts are regarded as some of their best clients because direct accounts don't have agencies that they are paying commission to, so dollar for dollar they are more profitable. Additionally, these stations have strong and at times very personal relationships with these clients, who they are continually *schmoozing*.

The morning of the golf outing, I got on the bus with about twelve other clients as we embarked on our forty-five-minute ride west to Ballybunion. On the bus, we were given our pairings. I was to play with two direct accounts of WSB (a Cox-owned property out of Atlanta) and their local sales manager, who I knew quite well. When we got to the first tee, there was a line of golfers waiting to start their round. We were introduced to our caddies and engaged in small talk while waiting our turn. In this type of situation, everyone is a little nervous for a host of reasons: unfamiliar course, unfamiliar playing partners, not to mention a gallery of about twenty other golfers watching to see you hit that perfect drive down the middle, or perhaps drive it out of bounds into the ominous graveyard to the right. When one of my playing partners, John Schafer (who was the CEO of dental clinics in Atlanta and Philadelphia), got on the tee box and started his pre-swing routine, I noticed that he was a left-handed golfer (can you say *déjà vu*?). Well, of course, I thought, "What a perfect time for a little *schtick*." I couldn't help myself. As a very serious John Schafer took a huge backswing, ready to hit that perfect drive down the middle on the first hole, I screamed out at the top of my lungs, "John!" Everyone, including my other playing partners, the caddies, the caddie master, and the gallery waiting for their turn at bat, had to be thinking, "What the _____?!" (you fill in the blank). John looked like he was in shock as I appeared to try and be of some assistance. In a very concerned tone I said, "John, you're standing on the wrong side of the ball." While it did get a pretty good laugh from all within an earshot, John on the other hand had to force a small closed-mouth grin.

At the time, we both had different impressions for what had just taken place. I thought he surely must've been a bit agitated, given the look on his face. John, however, conveyed to me later that it took the edge off the moment. He went on to tell me that he was quite nervous and that he had assumed from my outburst that I knew everybody and that I was just trying to break the ice.

That was the start of a great new relationship. When you walk a course playing golf with someone, you quickly get to know that person, especially when you're walking with caddies. People who know me know that I can be very engaging and open to everyone, including total strangers. As John and I walked the course, we covered several topics: family, politics, current events, and eventually, his business. We talked about media placement. We talked creative (John is actually the on-air talent for his dental locations). We talked about some back-end opportunities for his business, and I was curious as to whether he was taking advantage of them. With maybe three holes left, on the heels of one of my questions, he looked at me and said, "You and me are going to do business someday."

Now think about that. My intention was not to pick up an account that day, especially given the fact of how respectful I was that John's business was a direct account for the media company that was also hosting me and my wife. I was just doing what comes naturally for me—connecting with people. If you want to be great at connecting with people from all walks of life, please heed this advice: *Listen!* To hone your skills and to connect better with people, you have to be a great listener. On that very memorable round of golf at Ballybunion with John, I did very little of the talking. I asked some questions and John filled in all the blanks. Today I am proud to say that John is not just a client, but one of my best friends as well.

The Takeaway

Sam Snead, in my opinion, was right. Of all the hazards, fear is the worst, and fear of rejection by other people can stifle careers and hold you back in life. It doesn't matter who steps from what pedestal or how many zeros someone has in his or her bank account; we are all more alike than we are different. Remember that nobody is better than you or more special than you. Too many times we allow ourselves to be intimidated by other people. The insecurities we have, *we* have created, and they exist only in our minds. When you learn to overcome this fear of people and intimidation by others, "You're gonna need a bigger boat." (*Jaws*, 1975)

*This resort has recently undergone a $40 million renovation that includes a world-class spa, a new Tom Fazio golf course and a new wing of forty-two rooms, increasing the total to 104 guest rooms.

Chapter Seven

THE "WHAT-IF" SYNDROME

"Life is either a daring adventure...
or nothing at all."

— HELEN KELLER

Living life to its full potential is relative. For some, it means nothing more than sitting in the grandstands and watching the parade as it passes by. For others, it's far more than that. It's about allowing yourself not only to dream, but to act on those dreams. Stepping outside the proverbial "comfort zone" where you're not in control can be unsettling, even downright scary. How many times have you thought about doing something that you knew you had the God-given talent to do, but you didn't do it? The doubts and fears that take root in our lives are the result of what I call the "What-If Syndrome." What if this happens? What if *that* happens? What if my family thinks it's a bad idea? What if my friends think it's a bad idea? Or worst of all, what if I fail?

I won't say that I'm so reckless when it comes to stepping outside my comfort zone that I throw caution to the wind. I'm never going to bungee-jump off the Golden Gate Bridge, but I will tell you this: my life has been enriched by taking the fear of failure off the table. I've never really thought about whether I could or couldn't do something. If I thought it was something I wanted to do or something I could do, I just went out and gave it a shot.

Several years ago, a good friend of mine named Steve Chapman presented me with a challenge. Steve was the president and co-founder of *duPont Registry* magazine. We were sitting in his office one afternoon when he told me he had just signed up to run in the Marine Corps Marathon in six months in Washington, D.C. Steve was a natural athlete and had run many marathons before, including the New York Marathon twice, as well as the Boston Marathon twice. All that seemed pretty daunting to me, as the longest I'd ever run was a single mile in high school gym class. A marathon, on the other hand, is 26.2 miles.

Steve was especially excited about this marathon due to its taking place in Washington, D.C. The Marine Corps Marathon was established in 1976, and today is the fourth largest in the United States and the ninth largest in the world. With a field of thirty thousand runners, the Marine Corps Marathon takes runners on a breathtaking journey through some of the most historical sites anywhere in the world. The race's course includes running by the Capitol building, the Lincoln Memorial, the Washington Monument, the Kennedy Center, the Martin Luther King Jr. Memorial, and the Smithsonian Institution. It ends dramatically too, with an uphill run to the finish line at the U.S. Marine Corps War Memorial.

I told Steve that I would like to run a marathon like that at some time in my life. That was all Steve needed to hear. He immediately taunted me with laugher. "Cody, you couldn't run a marathon," he said. "That's 26.2 miles." Without missing a beat, he bet me one hundred dollars that I couldn't run and finish a race like the Marine Corps Marathon, fully expecting me to never take his wager. I immediately answered yes to his challenge, even though I'd given no real thought to the grueling undertaking that training for such a race would become.

Now I was stuck. My pride on the line, I quickly learned that there is nothing casual about preparing for a marathon. I was a complete novice to the running world and knew I had my work cut out for me. I realized that if I wanted to do it, I would need some help. At Steve's suggestion, I reached out to Jeff Galloway, an Olympian runner living in Atlanta. Jeff had a book on the market called *Galloway's Book on Running*, which I purchased. I then called him to see if he'd be interested in helping me out personally! Surprisingly, he liked the idea and agreed to help me, the poor, out-of-shape soul that I was, for a modest fee. Jeff really took his task to heart, setting me up with a new diet heavy on carbs, as well as a running schedule that would have me training right up to two weeks before the marathon date.

One thing in my favor was a perfect place to train. Lake Hollingsworth was and still is one of Lakeland's treasured landmarks. Named after John Henry Hollingsworth, one of Lakeland's early pioneers, the 2.8-mile, 350-acre lake allowed me to enjoy one of the most scenic routes anywhere. Maybe running along paths with such incredible views of Florida Southern College, with buildings designed by the late Frank Lloyd Wright, and by million-dollar homes, various wildlife, as well as the Lakeland Yacht Club would make my training less burdensome.

I remember my first attempt at trying to run around that lake like it was yesterday. I got up around 4:30 a.m., which was to be my new routine for the next several months. Then I drove down to the lake, which was about a mile from my home. As I started that first run, I realized that not only was I completely out of shape, but that I also suffered from what they call "deceptive" speed. Apparently, I was a whole lot slower than I had thought.

When I got to the halfway point of my first mile, I thought I was dying. My 182-pound body was panting so badly, I felt like a big, fat, worn-out English bulldog looking for his bowl of water. I couldn't even run the second half of the first mile, so I walked it instead. Occasionally, I tried to muster the courage to run again, but I'd only last about thirty seconds. What had I gotten myself into? Had I completely lost my mind? How on earth was I going to run 26.2 miles when I couldn't successfully run one mile?

My first thought was to write Steve a check for a hundred bucks and go back to bed. I didn't, though. I decided to tough it out, and after my first week of training, I was able to jog around the lake without stopping. It probably isn't fair to call what I was doing "jogging." It was more of a slow, lumbering, lethargic walk-jog, at a tortoise-like fifteen-minute per mile pace. Some people can crawl faster than that. I do remember feeling a sense of pride, though, as I looked out over the lake and realized I had made it around the three miles of Lake Hollingsworth without stopping.

Well, as the weeks and months went by, I continued to build up my stamina and jog around the lake without stopping. I made it around two times, then three times, then five times. Two weeks before the event, I was able to run around Lake Hollingsworth non-stop eight times! That was twenty-three miles. And with my new physique of a svelte 159 pounds, I was ready for the marathon.

Come marathon weekend, my wife Phyllis, my nine-year-old son Cody Jr., and I headed to D.C., where we met up with Phyllis's parents, who happened to live there. We also connected with Steve and his wife, Liz. On Sunday, the day of the marathon, the temperature was a perfect forty-two degrees, and I was ready to complete this momentous milestone in my life. About thirty minutes before the race, an announcement was made that really bothered me. Runners would be grouped according to their qualifying speeds, so that meant that the fastest runners got to start in the front. Then, according to speed, runners would be staggered throughout, with the slowest runners starting the race at the end of the line.

With seventeen thousand runners, and me having beginner status, I was relegated to the very back of the line. That meant I would begin my run at least a half-mile behind the runners at the front of the line. It was then I decided to break out of my comfort zone and go to the very front of the line along with my fellow world-class marathoners. Even at my new weight of 159, I wasn't fooling anybody, and these elite runners were definitely not intimidated by me. Still, when the starting gun went off, I was up front, and for maybe one whole second, I was leading the Marine Corps Marathon. In a matter of a few seconds, however, there were hundreds of runners ahead of me. After about two minutes, there I was alongside runners of my own speed at the end of the line.

Because of Jeff and his coaching, at the age of forty-two, I was able to finish the Marine Corps Marathon in four hours and forty-three minutes. That was ahead of Vice President Al Gore (age forty-nine), who ran it in 4:54, and behind Oprah (age forty), who finished at 4:29. Because of my good friend Steve Chapman and his jovial prodding, I accomplished something I never would have tried otherwise, and for that I am very grateful.

Stepping outside one's comfort zone is for the most part a conscious decision. Running a marathon on a bet was a challenge I accepted and then met head-on. There are times and circumstances in our lives, however, that put us in uncomfortable situations or uncharted waters—situations where we've already made a commitment, then start to have second thoughts because the road ahead seems too daunting.

My mother reminded me on more than one occasion when I was growing up of what my grandfather Frank Cody used to say: "Don't expect anything out of a man until he's thirty." Don't tell that to Facebook founder Mark Zuckerberg, Starbucks Chairman Howard Schultz, rapper Jay-Z, or fashion designer Ralph Lauren. They all became huge successes before age thirty. Sure, there are many exceptions to my grandfather's saying, but by the time I was twenty-five, I was already programmed and knew that if I wanted to try something truly daring in my life, I only had about five years to do it.

At the age of twenty-five, even though I was making a good living in the car business, I was very certain that I did not want to make the automobile business my lifelong career. I had spent four years working my way through college, and I just felt I was destined for something greater in life, or at least something more meaningful. *Something greater? Something more meaningful?* I got it! Why not stand-up comedy? As crazy as that seemed to many family and friends, I felt like it was a very rational avenue to pursue.

As early as I can remember, I had always made people laugh and, yes, I was definitely the class clown. Attending a new high school for my senior year forced me to harness some of my craziness (*some*...I still bark on planes) and to focus on newfound talents, including public speaking, as well as more refined ways of showcasing my talents. After only six weeks at my new high school, nominations for senior superlatives were being taken, and I was blown away when I found myself on a list of four for "Most Talented." I remember thinking, "How is this possible?" I hardly knew anyone at this school, and I was nominated. Well, I wasn't voted "Most Talented," but later in the year I lived up to the nomination by having the opportunity to emcee two of the school's biggest events: "Spring Follies," attended by local dignitaries including the mayor himself, and "Fractured Flicks."

At the University of South Florida, I majored in communications (advertising & PR), but a close look at my transcript would reveal that I had almost as many speech credits as I did in communications. I won a statewide contest for humorous speaking in my junior year, and in the first quarter of my senior year I petitioned to take a 400-level speech performance course, even though I wasn't a speech major. The class was taught by Dr. Bernard Downs, who not only accepted me in his class, but also later became one of my biggest boosters. There were about fifteen people in the class, and they were all speech or theatre majors. My first day of class, it became apparent that I was clearly the outsider, because everyone was already very chummy with one another. I wasn't readily accepted into their little clique. Until I proved that I was worthy to be in their company, the best I could expect was a polite "hello" and a polite "goodbye."

Our first assignment was to write and deliver a ten-minute persuasive speech. With a week to prepare, I decided to take a humorous approach and write a sales pitch with fast, hard-hitting dialogue that I would deliver in a comedic voice similar to Art Fern, Johnny Carson's "Tea Time Movie" host character from the *Tonight Show*. And what would I be selling? A "do-it-yourself" vasectomy kit—only $14.95! I'll spare you the "operation" part of the skit where I talked about cutting the vas deferens, thus stopping the sperm from traveling through the urethra, and go right to the opening:

> "Are you tired of using those same old contraceptive methods? You know, the ones that are so tiresome, burdensome, and usually carry some degree of risk? Well, what's a frustrated couple to do? Why not do what so many Americans are doing and turn to the one sure way to rid yourself of those pesky little creatures? *Vasectomy*, friends…yes, *vasectomy*— the least expensive, most reliable form of birth control is now available in this *do-it-yourself kit* for only $14.95…yes, friends, for $14.95 you receive antiseptic, gauze, scalpel…and while they last a "Win Button" from the Association of Voluntary Sterilization."

During my presentation I even got off track a few times with some ad-libs like this one: "Get up here, young man, and put those big sperm ducts on the chopping block and show these folks just how painless this operation can be!"

After the first two minutes, my classmates were rolling in the aisle. I then realized that I was now part of the club. Professor Downs, who was very talented in his own right, thought I should change majors and go into theatre. That year I got the lead role in one of the school's major productions, *Two Short Stories*, by Kurt Vonnegut. It was a great opportunity for me to be both the narrator *and* the lead actor. During the show, I would step out of the scene and talk to the audience to explain something while the rest of the cast stayed still (also known as an aside). I would then walk back into the scene and resume acting with the rest of the cast. The production was a huge success and planted a seed in Professor Downs's mind that I might have bigger roles ahead of me.

After graduating from college, I was well into my first month at the automobile dealership when I got a call from Professor Downs, who said he had something exciting to share with me and suggested we have lunch. While I couldn't imagine what the excitement was all about, I had enough respect for the guy who was my biggest (and maybe only) fan to take the time to meet. His next big production was going to be *Dracula*, and he wanted me for the lead. As he was talking and encouraging me, I was getting caught up in the moment. I felt that I could knock it out of the park, but then reality set in. For the first time in my life I could finally see some daylight at the end of the financial tunnel.

As I mentioned before, when I graduated from college, I didn't have two nickels to rub together, and the thought of living the life of a college student again was not something I was looking forward to. I was a rising star at the dealership, leading the board in sales, and in possession of my brand new Chevrolet Impala. If I had agreed to take on the role, it would've been an eight-week commitment. To stay on track, I knew it was not something I could do, so I reluctantly told Professor Downs that I would have to decline.

I wasn't lacking in self-confidence, so for all the above-mentioned reasons, I felt that I had the background and the talent to take a shot at one of the more insecure and unpredictable careers one could choose in life: stand-up comedy. Making a living doing stand-up was a short-term goal. My long-range goal was to get it going and see what other doors might open. Today, a young and talented comic can make a living and hone their skills in comedy clubs until their "big break." When I was embarking on what was to be a wild ride, young stand-ups often worked for free, hoping for the opportunity to get the right exposure in front of the right people.

Three months into my new and not-so-lucrative career in comedy, I landed my first paid gig. I was booked at the Serena Hotel in St. Petersburg, Florida, by a local Tampa talent agency. The hotel has since been torn down, but at the time it was a very upscale destination catering to an older and wealthy clientele from the Northeast. I wasn't given a lot of information from the agent, only that they brought in local entertainers a few times a year during the winter months to perform for this *crème de la crème* audience. I arrived at the hotel in my evening best—a loud plaid sport coat that I was certain would be the fashion statement of the evening. And it was.

As I walked through the lobby of the hotel, I almost couldn't believe my eyes. I was in the midst of the largest group of octogenarians I had ever witnessed in one place, and they weren't dressed in their Sunday best. Instead, they were all dressed in formal attire that I was sure they didn't have to rent—the men in their tuxedos and the women in their long evening gowns. "Dear God," I thought, "this cannot be the group I'm about to get in front of." Then, out of nowhere, came the woman who was in charge, dressed in a full-length formal gown, of course. *Charming* is not the word I would use to describe this woman. She looked, acted, and moved like Cruella de Vil, the lead character from the Disney animated feature *101 Dalmatians.*

She obviously knew who I was, and she was not interested in any niceties or formal introductions. Getting very close to my face with a hushed tone and bulging eyes, she wanted to know why I wasn't wearing a tuxedo. I wanted so badly to tell her that this was now the second time my dry cleaner had lost my tux, but nothing about her suggested that she was in the mood for any one-liners. The truth was that my agent said nothing about the affair being a formal event, which is precisely what I conveyed to Miss Congeniality. So, with those same bulging eyes and a short guttural response, she stormed off in the opposite direction. I had more than an hour before show time, so I figured I could at least find the ballroom and meet some of the other entertainers. What happened next was horrifying. In fact, if given the option, I would have preferred a one-on-one "Spin the Bottle" marathon with Cruella.

There, in front of this grand entrance to the ballroom, was a ten-foot vertical sign, "TONIGHT: COMEDIAN AND IMPRESSIONIST CODY LOWRY." I was the only entertainer scheduled for the evening. *Wow*…talk about being outside your comfort zone! For a split-second, I thought that it had to be a *Candid Camera* moment, except there was no Allen Funt around. As I stood there in shock, a guy came up to me and introduced himself. He was the bass player in the quartet as well as the emcee for the night. He was very helpful, giving me the me the lowdown on what to expect from the octogenarians, which included, "Make sure to speak up." No kidding!

The moment finally arrived. I was introduced and welcomed with polite applause that made me think for a moment that maybe this would work out just fine. This was not a Sun City or The Villages crowd. This group was twenty years removed, with at least every other table having a walker parked close by. Don't get me wrong—I loved the older generation then and still do today, but was I really the right fit? Where was Guy Lombardo when you needed him? It wasn't like I had a lot of years under my belt with an ensemble of comedy material, where I could easily pivot from one routine to another. No, I had a tight twenty-five minutes and, as good as I thought it was, it proved to be a bit off the mark in front of this particular audience. My performance started out well as I opened with some of my best impressions—John Wayne, Jimmy Stewart, Richard Nixon, Jack Webb, Ed Sullivan, and even Sullivan's adorable little mouse Topo Gigio. I seemed to be doing just fine and everyone appeared to be having a good time. That is, until I used the "V" word.

Now, I've never had to resort to any material that was vulgar or off-color in order to get a laugh, and this night was going to be no different. Or so I thought. After my impressions, I segued into my vasectomy routine that had been such a big hit with my college buds and had worked great with my previous non-paid engagements. I figured it would work here too. After the opening lines, I knew something was very wrong, and it just went downhill from there.

"Are you tired of using those same old contraceptive measures… you know, the ones that are so tiresome, burdensome, and usually carry with it some degree of risk?"

Excluding myself and the quartet behind me, it had to have been fifty years since anyone in that ballroom was the least bit interested or concerned about the perils of contraception.

"Why not do what so many Americans are doing and turn to the one sure way to rid yourself of those pesky little creatures… *Vasectomy*, friends…yes, *vasectomy!*"

Judging their reactions, you'd think I had just dropped the F-bomb! I actually saw women covering their ears, fearing I might say the "V" word again. Still, I plunged ahead…

"The least expensive, most reliable form of birth control is now available to you in this *do-it-yourself kit* for only $14.95!"

At this point, many in the audience were shuffling away with their walkers, apparently offended by my humor, and heading to the nearest exit. All of a sudden, the emcee came up behind me and said that it might be best if I left the stage. Leave the stage? I may have been new to the world of stand-up comedy, but I knew one thing for sure—I was *not* about to leave that stage. I immediately shifted back to more impressions, finishing with Elvis Presley and a John F. Kennedy that most of my remaining audience seemed to enjoy. That night was a great learning experience for me. Number one: know thy audience. And, yes, learning that I was the sole entertainer that night forced me to step outside my comfort zone. Little did I know that I was just months away from one of the biggest outside-my-comfort-zone moments in my life.

I was only six months into my stand-up endeavor when I decided the best way to fine-tune my craft was to head out to Las Vegas, where comedians quickly learn to sink or swim. Through a connection in Fort Lauderdale, I was introduced to a Las Vegas comedian named Jackie Gayle. He was kind enough to spend a couple of hours with me sharing his sage advice and thoughts on how I might break into the business in Sin City. Gayle was a comedian and actor who had made an incredible living opening shows for some of the biggest names in show business, like Tony Bennett, Tom Jones, Paul Anka, and Tina Turner. In his mid-fifties he built an impressive career appearing in such movies as *Tin Man*, *Mr. Saturday Night*, and *Bulworth*, as well as twenty Dean Martin Celebrity Roast specials. With his Brooklyn accent and noticeable lisp, Mr. Gayle didn't try and paint me a rosy picture, explaining that it was going to take a lot of hard work and to not expect any miracles overnight.

I was about three months away from heading out to Las Vegas when I decided to visit New York City. I didn't have the resources to sustain me for any length of time in the Big Apple, but I wanted to get to the city in hopes that I could get up and do a set at Budd Friedman's famous Improv or Rick Newman's Catch A Rising Star. The Improv was started in 1963 by Budd Friedman, who was aptly known as the "Godfather of Comedy." Located on West 44th Street in Hell's Kitchen, the Improv was responsible for launching the careers of George Carlin, Steve Martin, Jerry Seinfeld, Drew Carey, Robert Klein, and many more. Newman's Catch A Rising Star opened in December 1975 and was located on 1st Avenue between 77th and 78th Streets. The club started out as a variety club but soon became the destination for up-and-coming and established comedians like Ray Romano, Robin Williams, Billy Crystal, Adam Sandler, Chris Rock, Richard Lewis, and so many more, including Larry David (who I think is one of the funniest people on the planet today). How was I going to get myself on stage at one of these iconic clubs?

The first night I went to the Improv, the place was packed with a pretty hip crowd that appeared to be having a good time. I'm not sure if I was just in awe, overwhelmed, intimidated, or all the above that night, but I didn't try to reach out to anyone. The following night, I headed uptown to Catch a Rising Star, where it was standing-room only. I really didn't think there was much of a chance of getting up on stage that night, but when I talked to the guy who seemed to be running things and told him my story, he put me on the list. Wow! Was this really happening? I waited from the bar and watched some very funny comedians do their acts. About two hours later, I was alerted that I was up next. This was my big moment!

The comedian I was to follow was in the middle of his set when I was approached again and told that another guy was going to go on ahead of me. His name was Tom Dreesen, a well-established, successful comedian who was going to appear on *The Tonight Show* the following evening and wanted to try out some new material. Dreesen had toured with Frank Sinatra for fourteen years and throughout his career had appeared on *The Tonight Show* fifty-plus times. I wasn't the least bit disappointed. If anything, it added to the excitement of that evening and drove home the reality that this venue was at the top of the food chain when it came to comedy clubs. Tom was soon introduced, and shockingly, he bombed. For whatever reason, Tom was not connecting. Standing in the wings, I felt very uncomfortable for him, which was a surreal moment for me. About halfway through his routine, Tom put the microphone back in the stand, apologized to the audience, and said that he was going to work on some different material for his appearance on *The Tonight Show*. Very quickly after, I was introduced. "From Tampa, Florida, give a big hand for comedian and impressionist— Cody Lowry!" And there I was, running up to the stage, about to address this group of very comedy-savvy people. I was probably too scared to be nervous, but with my high-energy style, I immediately started to connect with the audience. I led with impressions, including a Jack Webb routine, did a funny bit on diaper rash, and finished with my standard go-to—the Do-It-Yourself Vasectomy Kit For $14.95. When it was over, I received a big applause and it felt great. And while the William Morris Agency wasn't waiting in the wings with a contract, I felt like I had held my own at the most prestigious comedy venue in America.

I wouldn't characterize my performance at Catch a Rising Star as stepping outside my comfort zone. It was the career I was pursuing, after all. But what happened next certainly was! My second day in New York City, I got the crazy idea that I should audition for *Saturday Night Live*. So, I called the offices at 30 Rockefeller Plaza and asked who was in charge of new talent, to which they gave me the name of John Head. They didn't immediately put me through to his office, instead telling me that he wasn't available and that I should call back. Surprisingly, when I called again later that afternoon, I got right through. I explained to Mr. Head that I was a comedian and could do impressions, including a great Jimmy Carter. I figured that could only increase my odds, since the show was known for its political humor and Carter had a good chance of becoming our next president. I went on to explain that I was only in town for a short period of time and would love an opportunity to audition for the show.

I was pretty sure I wasn't following protocol and didn't know what to expect, so I was shocked when Mr. Head explained that he was tied up at that moment but to try him back the next day. If that was a brush-off, it sure didn't feel like it! But when I tried the next day, it was impossible to get him back on the phone. After at least three more attempts of wearing his secretary out, I decided to try calling him at home that night. Bingo! He had a listed number. When he answered the phone, I almost couldn't believe it. In an excited tone I said, "Mr. Head, this is Cody Lowry." It was apparent from his response that he wasn't as excited as I was. Surprised, maybe, but definitely not excited. "You are unbelievable," he said. But, being the gentleman that he was, he gave me a time for the following day to stop by for a quick meeting.

That night I couldn't sleep. I kept thinking, "Wow—I'm going to audition for the hottest comedy show in the country!" Then I began to get nervous. Who was I kidding? Up until this time, the biggest thing I had ever auditioned for was a part in a college play. I didn't have an agent, and as confident as I was with my raw talent, that's exactly what I had—*raw* talent without any real experience. *Raw* talent without the benefit of paying my dues. Talk about stepping outside my comfort zone!

The next day I headed for NBC Studios at Rockefeller Plaza, where *Saturday Night Live* was taped. As I was going up in the elevator, I thought, "What a surreal moment...is this really happening?" I knew I was nervous because I really needed to go to the bathroom, but when those elevator doors opened, a sense of calm overtook me. I felt right at home and ready to charge. It wasn't long after I arrived that I was ushered into a room. Shortly after, John Head came in and introduced himself. My immediate thought was that John was a real gentleman. As unorthodox as my approach had been setting up this audition, he couldn't have made me feel more comfortable. I was surprised that it was just the two of us in that room, and when he asked me to go to the front of the room to a platform, I knew I had only one person to impress to have any chance of getting my big break.

I did about fifteen minutes of my best material, including my standard vasectomy bit, my best impressions, and my Jimmy Carter impersonation. It was 1976, and Jimmy Carter was running for president against sitting President Gerald Ford. It looked like the former governor of Georgia had a real shot at the big prize, and as far as I knew, there was nobody on the national stage impersonating Carter. As I was doing my routine, I felt I was connecting with John. While he wasn't falling on the floor with laughter, he had a big, genuine smile on his face. I finished my routine and Mr. Head excused himself. When he returned a short time later, two other men were with him and he asked me to do the Carter bit again. When I finished, the other two gentlemen (to whom I was never formally introduced) simply left the room. Mr. Head told me he thought I had nailed the Carter impression and said, "Let's see if he does in fact become president. In the meantime, I'll try to catch you around the city." He must have forgotten the fact that I was only in town for a week, so there was no chance he was going to catch me around the city.

I headed back to Florida, fully intending to move to Las Vegas in four months, but as fate would have it, I never made it. Instead, I was lured back into the automobile business with a very lucrative offer, and to be perfectly honest, I have no regrets. As confident as I was that I would've been successful, any fame or fortune I may have found pales in comparison to what I have today—a wonderful family, including eleven grandchildren!

The Takeaway

As author Rose Tremain once said, "Life is not a dress rehearsal." I believe that. Let's face it—no one is going to live forever, and what little time you have left on this Earth, whether you're twenty-five or ninety-five, should be spent living life to the fullest. One surefire way to do so is to take a walk on the wild side and step outside your comfort zone. Remember, it's never too late to take the plunge! Ray Kroc didn't buy out the McDonald brothers until he was fifty-nine. Colonel Sanders didn't start the Kentucky Fried Chicken franchise until he was sixty-five. Grandma Moses didn't start painting until she was seventy-five. Put yourself out there and stay on the stage, or better yet, take the advice of Mae West: "You only live once, but if you do it right, once is enough."

Chapter Eight

THE SPOILS OF
SCHMOOZING

"Seek opportunities to show you care. The smallest gestures often make the biggest difference."

— Coach JOHN WOODEN

There is a Gaelic proverb that states, "There are no pockets in a shroud." When our time comes and we leave this world, the overwhelming majority of us will not be remembered for the worldly possessions we leave behind. We probably won't be remembered for our famous or infamous lives. And there's a good chance we won't be remembered for our wonderful philanthropic giving. We might, however, be remembered by family, friends, and acquaintances for our selfless acts of kindness—sometimes random and spontaneous (*schmoozing*)—that had an impact on the lives of others. For me, life has been a smorgasbord of these little events, and sometimes I have been the recipient of such spontaneous behavior.

Several years ago, I was playing golf with a lot of pain in my feet and struggling with my walking. At the time, I didn't know that I had *plantar fasciitis*. The pain seemed to get worse with each hole I played, and my golf partners could see how I was really struggling. I was actually considering heading back to the clubhouse when Chuck Massic, the least likely of our group, asked what was wrong. I say "least likely" because I didn't know Chuck all that well, and when he was on the course, he was totally self-absorbed with himself and his game.

I tried shrugging it off, but Chuck was persistent in questioning me. After a quick explanation, he gave me a quick diagnosis—*plantar fasciitis*—something from which Chuck also suffered. What happened next blew me away. Without hesitation, Chuck took off his golf shoes, removed the inserts he was wearing, and gave them to me. As hard as I tried to reject this kind gesture, Chuck was adamant. He wouldn't take no for an answer, so a few minutes later I was wearing his inserts. Wow! Was I wrong about Chuck! Beneath his standoffish and often aloof veneer was a person who was anything but. And, in fact, he was a person who knew how to *schmooze* in his own little way. I might someday forget an incredible chip shot or that phenomenal forty-foot putt I made to win a hole, but I will never forget that day and Chuck's act of kindness.

Selfless acts of kindness are done without regard to what we might receive in return. It's about doing the right thing at the right time to help others. Because I travel for business (and, yes, because of my affable, outgoing personality), I get more opportunities than most people to reach out, and if I'm lucky, to have a positive effect on the people I meet. In life, when we show people we care, the rewards can be quite remarkable.

Unless you have been affiliated with a winning NFL team, there's a good chance you don't have a Super Bowl ring. Well, I do, and I can tell you that it wasn't because I wanted one, or that I asked for one, or even that it was some deep-seated desire of mine. Today I am convinced that the only reason I am a proud recipient of a Super Bowl ring is because I had an opportunity to show someone that I genuinely cared. Who decided to bestow this honor? None other than NFL Hall of Famer and colorful winning coach of Super Bowl IV, the late Hank Stram. Considered a football legend and one of the most motivational coaches in the history of the NFL, Coach Stram had the honor to coach two Super Bowl games as head coach for the Kansas City Chiefs in the AFL (American Football League). In 1967, the Chiefs played the Green Bay

Packers in Super Bowl I, with the Packers winning 35–10. In 1970, the Chiefs won the AFC and went to Super Bowl IV, where they beat the Minnesota Vikings 23–7.

It was during this game that Stram became the first professional coach to wear a microphone during a championship game for NFL Films. Stram's recorded comments from that game have become classics:

> "Just keep matriculating the ball down the field, boys."

> "Mister Ref, how could all six of you miss that play?"

> "Sixty-five toss power trap."

> "Kassulke was running around there like it was a Chinese fire drill."

The Super Bowl victory was the second in a row by a team from the AFL and added credibility to the newer league. After his coaching career, Stram carved out a nice living broadcasting for CBS on both TV and radio. His longest-running gig was on radio doing *Monday Night Football* for eighteen years with sidekick Jack Buck. At the time, the radio broadcast drew incredible ratings, mostly due to many listeners turning off the sound on their TVs while watching the games to listen to Hank and Jack instead of the bombastic voice of Howard Cosell on TV.

I first met Coach Stram at a WTOG-TV party for the Tampa Bay Buccaneers in 1983. Stram had then been hired by the station to call the Bucs preseason games. It was a pretty good local gig that gave Coach an opportunity to get ready for his NFL regular season job on CBS with Jack Buck. My wife and I were already at our table when in he came in. Talk about a flamingo! Stram was wearing a bright orange jacket—the only thing missing was lights! When he walked into the room, I knew exactly who he was (by this time I had seen the NFL clip two or three times), and I said to my wife, "Honey, that's Hank Stram!" To which she immediately replied, "That's the ugliest jacket I've ever seen."

That was the start of a twenty-year friendship that to this day is a very special part of my history. We played golf together, we did TV commercials, and for two years, he was the honorary chairman of my golf tournament, following Sparky Anderson. We enjoyed each other's company, and eventually our wives, both named Phyllis, became friends.

One thing that always concerned me was whether the coach was doing OK financially. He always seemed to be hustling with this deal or that deal, and because of his star power everybody wanted a piece of him. One evening we were having dinner together and he was talking about making some deal, which prompted me to cautiously ask him a question that had been on my mind for several years. "Coach," I said, "are you doing OK financially?" Almost without a pause, Coach started to laugh, and he asked me what had brought that on. When I shared my concerns and observations over the years, he gave me a big, warm smile and told me he was doing much better than *OK*. He went on to explain that years earlier, Chiefs owner Lamar Hunt had made some great investments for him, and with his CBS contract he had no concerns. It was at that moment that Coach Stram became somewhat serious, looked at me, and said, "Cody, I'm gonna make a big man out of you." I had absolutely no idea where he was going with that. Then he said, "How would you like a Super Bowl ring?" In all the years the coach and I had been friends (probably fifteen at this point) never did I think about such an honor, but with absolutely no hesitation I said, "Are you kidding? Absolutely!" For some reason, I had assumed that he had an extra ring at his house or in a safe deposit box someplace, but to my surprise he ordered it through the ring company that had a contract with the NFL. As you might expect, the ring company was very protective of their account. I later found out that they actually called Lamar Hunt for permission to make the ring.

Years later, my wife and I, along with Monsignor Caulfield, who was also a friend of the Strams, were spending a short weekend in New Orleans when we got word that Coach Stram was taken by ambulance to the hospital in Covington, Louisiana, where he and his wife lived. With Covington being about an hour drive across Lake Pontchartrain from New Orleans, Monsignor and I were immediately off to the hospital, hoping and praying for the best. When we arrived, we were met by Hank's wife Phyllis, and Dale, one of their four sons. The mood was somber, and by the looks on their faces, the situation was serious.

When Monsignor and I walked into the room, Coach seemed to be in a deep sleep and was resting peacefully. After conferring with Phyllis, Monsignor, who had been in this situation hundreds of times, decided that it would be best to administer the last rites. In Roman Catholicism, the last rites are the last prayers given to someone of faith shortly before death. So, with Phyllis, Dale, Monsignor, and myself at the coach's side, the last rites were administered. Afterwards, Phyllis stepped out of the room and I immediately followed. While she was a devout Catholic and was obviously upset, she was in total control. It was then that I chose to address something that had been on my mind ever since I had arrived at the hospital. In addition to Dale, the Strams had four other children: Mary, Julia, Henry, Gary, and Stu. I told Phyllis that I would like to have my Super Bowl ring sent to her so that she might give it to one of the boys. She seemed a bit surprised but responded quickly, "Cody, the boys have their rings." Both she and her husband knew the importance of his gift, and at that moment, the magnitude of it registered with me.

As I work on this chapter, it's football season—usually a time when I wear that ring. Three weeks ago, during a business trip in Detroit, as my driver was taking me to my hotel, we talked about football. (For the record, do not get into a sports trivia contest with anyone from Detroit or Philadelphia, because you will lose. They not only know their team's players and stats; they know *your* team's players and stats as well!) Surprisingly, my driver's favorite team wasn't the Detroit Lions. Being from Missouri, this older gentleman was a die-hard Kansas City Chiefs fan. When I told him that Hank Stram had a Super Bowl ring made for me, he was almost beside himself. Then I remembered that I had the ring packed away in my luggage and asked if he wanted to see it. Then he really went crazy! We took pictures of me wearing the ring and of him wearing the ring, as well as close-up shots of the ring. You would've thought I was showing him the Hope Diamond! Now, I can't promise you a Super Bowl ring, but this I will promise: show people that you genuinely care, and you will not only enrich their lives but your own as well.

OK, so what do Magic Johnson and Cody Lowry have in common? Answer: we both carried the torch in the 2002 Salt Lake City Olympic Torch Relay. I recently viewed a TV program on the life of Magic Johnson. The show was filmed at his home, and during the end of the segment, out comes Magic carrying his torch, which was mounted on a large wooden plaque (I have one too!). He told the interviewer that it was his most prized possession. Magic Johnson had an opportunity to carry the torch because he had five NBA championships, three NBA MVP Awards, nine NBA Finals appearances, twelve All-Star games, and ten All-NBA First and Second Team nominations. Johnson became a two-time inductee (Los Angeles Lakers; 1992 Summer Olympics Dream Team) into the Basketball Hall of Fame, and on and on and on. In short, Magic Johnson carried the torch because he is one of the greatest basketball players that ever played the game. I, on the other hand, had an opportunity to carry the torch because I was there for someone when they reached out to me.

It really doesn't matter what field you're in. We all meet people along the way who for one reason or another just seem to stand out. I first met Kurt Ritter (now chairman and CEO of Saatchi & Saatchi L.A. and chairman of Saatchi & Saatchi Canada) when he was the Southeast zone manager for Chevrolet based in Tampa. Because my agency was also based in Tampa and represented Tier 2 Chevrolet Dealer groups (all the Chevrolet dealers in one marketing trade area), Kurt and I got to know each other better than I otherwise would have had the agency not been located in Tampa. As zone manager for the Southeast, Kurt was in charge of all aspects of Chevrolet business in a five-state area: sales, service, distribution, and customer service. After working with Kurt for just a short period of time, it was my observation that he was on the fast track and wouldn't be a resident of Florida for very long. He was smart, hard-working, had strong communication skills, was a good listener, and was absolutely great at dealing with people. Sure enough, it wasn't long before Kurt landed a very big position with Chevrolet in Detroit, eventually rising to the position of general marketing manager for Chevrolet Motor Division, heading up all of Chevrolet's national advertising and marketing. Even though Kurt (at least from my vantage point) was now in the big leagues, we continued to be friends, seeing each other at marketing meetings and, on occasion, playing a round of golf.

Kurt had been in Detroit for several years when I got a call from him regarding his son Andy. Andy had recently graduated from college and was living in Tampa but was struggling to find a position associated with his film and video major. Kurt asked me if

I had any leads for Andy, and I told him, "Absolutely!" Shortly after that, Andy reached out and we got together. I liked Andy immediately. With his All-American looks and a fire in his belly, he was ready to start his career and conquer the world. With the connections I had in the industry in Tampa, it was a good fit, and we began to network. We agreed that we would meet weekly to review our progress and pursue different avenues.

In the meantime, Andy was working at TGI Fridays to pay the bills. After three weeks of meetings and interviews and still not hitting pay dirt, I got a call from Andy. I could tell he was excited when he said he wanted to come by the office that afternoon. When he arrived, the excitement was evident by the indelible smile on his face.

"I got a job," he said.

"Wow, Andy, that's great news! Tell me more." I said.

"I got a job as a junior account executive with Campbell Ewald in Detroit."

Any level of excitement I had was now gone, and I almost couldn't believe my ears. "Campbell Ewald? You have got to be kidding!" I said. At the time, Campbell Ewald was the national ad agency for Chevrolet and the creative powerhouse who gave us one iconic advertising campaign after another, including "The Heartbeat of America;" "Baseball, Hot Dogs, Apple Pie;" and a campaign Kurt had actually worked on, "Chevrolet—Like a Rock." I said to Andy, "Why? This isn't what you want to do." He went on to tell me that he was tired of working at TGI Fridays and wanted to get a job. He could tell I wasn't happy with his decision, so I explained why. Campbell Ewald's biggest and longest-running account at the time was Chevrolet, and Kurt Ritter was very influential with the agency. I told Andy, "Please be patient, because today, tomorrow, next week, or next month your dad can pick up the phone and get you a position at that agency. Andy, please give yourself more time." I explained that his passion deserved a little patience, and that I would be doing him a great disservice by jumping on the Campbell Ewald bandwagon. That day, we parted on the same page, with Andy agreeing to put the Campbell Ewald position on hold to give his dream job more time. Almost a week to the day, I received a call from Andy, who let me know that he had landed a job in South Florida in his field, one that he had interviewed for some months earlier.

It wasn't long afterwards that I got another call from Andy letting me know that he was getting married and wanted me to come to the wedding in Spring Lake, New Jersey. My wife and I went to the wedding and had a great time. Not only did we get to see Andy and his bride walk down the aisle, but it gave us both an opportunity to bond with the whole Ritter family, including Kurt's wife, Patty.

After the wedding Kurt and I stayed in touch, and because Tampa was where his daughter and twin sons also lived, we would get together for a Tampa Bay Buccaneers game or a round of golf. In the fall of 2001, I was in my office in Tampa when Kurt called from Detroit to say he was headed to Tampa in the next few weeks. After we talked about maybe getting together for a Bucs game, he explained the reason for his call. Kurt wanted to know if I would like to carry the torch in the 2002 Winter Olympics to be held in Salt Lake City. Without hesitation, and without knowing the full extent of the honor I was being accorded, I immediately said yes. I had my choice of two cities: Los Angeles or Santa Fe. After discussing it with my wife, we chose Santa Fe. My first thought was that this was something I needed to start training for, but then found out that I'd only have to run with the torch for about 1,200 feet.

This was an honor that came out of left field. To this day I am convinced that had I not been available when Kurt called, or had he reached out to someone else to help Andy, I wouldn't have carried the torch in the 2002 Olympics. When you consider that Kurt was personal friends with the biggest and most successful Chevrolet dealers in the country, and personal friends with agency owners whose ad agencies eclipsed my shop in both size and billing, there can only be one answer as to why I was chosen: because I was there for someone when they reached out to me.

I'm not sure where I would be today without mentors in my life (Hugh Hoffman, chapter two; Dick Davis, chapter three). And I would be remiss if I didn't put on the list one of Tampa Bay's iconic advertising giants. Bob Faller, founder of FKQ Advertising in Clearwater, Florida, came to my aid on several occasions during my early years in the agency business. My first formal meeting with Bob (at the time, I addressed him as "Mr. Faller" and he immediately corrected me and said to call him "Bob") was in Paris, France, where we were both on a media trip. And a couple of years later, we met in Sydney, Australia. Bob was a certified A#1 *Schmoozer*, so much so that I, the guy that's literally writing the book on *schmoozing*, had nothing on him. On these trips, we talked shop, mostly with Bob doing the talking, as I did the listening. Several years later, Bob invited me to his office to discuss a possible merger of my company with another agency in the market. This was out of my wheelhouse, and frankly, I felt like a fish out of water. Once again, Bob was kind enough to share with me some sage advice and know-how that I desperately needed at the time. Few people make it to the top of their career without some incredible mentors in their life. Oprah Winfrey was mentored by the late author and poet Maya Angelou. Steve Jobs served as a mentor to Facebook CEO Mark Zuckerberg. Fashion designer Christian Dior mentored designer Yves St. Laurent. And former U.S. Secretary of State Colin Powell considered his father, Luther Powell, to be a great mentor in his life.

Helping people through their challenges is a way for me to give back. It inspires me when I watch mentees grow through life. The following poem appears in the *Handbook for Mentors and Mentees* for the Career Development Mentor Program at the University of Southern California:

My Mentor, My Friend

Thank you for allowing me
the opportunity
to learn from you
when I was seeking so much knowledge
when I was asking many questions
you patiently listened and answered accordingly
never showing signs of frustration

Thank you for taking the time
to show me the necessary skills today
that will lead me with confidence into tomorrow
for believing in me and having enough faith
to share your work
your dreams
and your vision

Thank you for accepting me as I am
with all my eagerness
and my sheer joy over the little things…
you never tried to squelch that spirit in me
Instead, you have encouraged that spirit
and for that, I do thank you

I realized the knowledge I need for work can be
learned anywhere,
taught by most anyone
but the life skills I needed that go along with it…

well, that would have to be taught by a very unique
individual
with a very special gift for giving
a gift of patience and understanding
that someone is you, my Mentor
and now, my friend

© THERESA GENTER

The Takeaway

So many times, we hear people say, "What goes around comes around," or "We reap what we sow," usually in a negative context. The same can be said about positive things too. Because of our own generous actions, we are rewarded when we least expect it. The spoils of *schmoozing* can be great. But life's greater rewards are reserved for those who demonstrate a commitment to be kind to others. I guess Lou Holtz said it best: "I follow three rules. Do the right thing. Do the best you can. And always show people you care."

Chapter Nine

SCHMOOZING FROM THE PODIUM

"All great speakers were bad speakers at first."

— Ralph Waldo Emerson

Stevie Wonder, born Stevland Hardaway Judkins (later changed to Morris), was clearly a child prodigy. Blind from birth and growing up in poverty, Stevie learned how to write music, play the piano, organ, and harmonica, and sing. By age twelve, he began his recording and performing career. Wolfgang Amadeus Mozart, Pablo Picasso, Tiger Woods...the list goes on and on of young people, usually under the age of ten, who displayed a prodigious ability in the arts, sciences, mathematics, or sports. The good news is that when it comes to public speaking, most of us don't need to be imbued with a special innate talent.

Public speaking, for the most part, is a learned ability that almost anyone (depending on how hard they work at it) can master. Unfortunately, getting up and addressing an audience is also one of life's greatest fears to many people. *Glossophobia* is the technical term for the fear of public speaking. If this is one of your dreaded aversions in life, you'll be happy to know that you're in good company. There was a time when one of the wealthiest people in the world was terrified of getting up and addressing a group of people. When he started out in business, self-made billionaire Warren Buffett would get ill at the very thought of getting up in front of a group to speak. Not until he enrolled in a Dale Carnegie class (still available in major markets throughout the country) was he able to conquer his fear of public speaking. World-renowned minister Joel Osteen gave his first sermon at age thirty-six and recalls being "scared to death." And would it surprise you to know that our third president, Thomas Jefferson, was terrified at the thought of public speaking? In fact, during his eight years as president, he only gave two speeches, and according to those present, they were delivered in such a low tone, he could hardly be heard. The good news is that with a little effort on your part, you can overcome this fear of speaking, and the pot of gold at the end of the rainbow can be overflowing.

Early in my career, I was invited to showcase my talents at the International Platform Association in Washington, D.C., an organization specializing in connecting speakers and audiences. It was there where I met two influential and lifelong friends: Robert Henry, a comedic inspirational speaker from Auburn, Alabama, and Nido Qubein, a businessman and motivational speaker from High Point, North Carolina. I remember watching Nido's performance like it was yesterday. At the time, he had to have been only twenty-four or twenty-five years old, and I thought to myself that this guy was very special. Of Lebanese and Jordanian descent, Nido's pronounced broken English and inspirational message left the audience, including me, spellbound. I wasn't sure where Nido was headed, but one thing I was sure of was that getting up in front of people would become a big part of his life. Well, the rest is history. Nido Qubein not only became the founder of the National Speakers Association but also has authored twelve motivational books and is currently the third-highest-paid college president in the country, at High Point University. In 2006, along with Oprah Winfrey and Starbucks founder Howard Schultz, Nido was inducted into the Horatio Alger Association, an honor bestowed on individuals who, despite adversities early in life, embrace the association's values, which include personal initiative, perseverance, leadership, a commitment to excellence, a belief in the free enterprise system, and the importance of higher education and community service. It's no wonder that part of the required curric-ulum today for every incoming freshman at High Point University is a class in persuasive speaking and presentation skills.

So, is there a pot of gold at the end of the rainbow if you learn how to be a great public speaker? Absolutely! Much of the success I have attained in my career I can attribute to getting up and speaking before wide and varied groups. Fundraisers, special events, pitching new business...I've done it all, including eulogies. For me, honing my speaking skills came early when it was a requirement as part of my job as the general sales manager for a very large Chevrolet dealership. I had to deliver a mandatory sales meeting at 8 a.m., five days a week, to forty car salesmen, who I knew would rather be sleeping than getting a quick motivational injection so early in the morning. It was, however, something I took very seriously. Long before the advent of the internet and Google, you could find me at my desk between 6:45 and 7 a.m. every weekday morning preparing for my upcoming speech, surrounded by motivational and inspirational books. I did my best to make sure my message was upbeat, often humorous, and always relevant. The experience I gained by giving those daily pep talks proved to be invaluable when I entered advertising, as well as when I opened my own agency several years later.

A big part of the ad agency business is presenting and pitching new business. I have always been very confident (without being cocky) that with the right client-focused preparation. I'd always have a good chance of winning their business. Because of my background, it was no surprise that almost 90 percent of my agen-cy's billing was in automotive advertising. In 1992, our shop was representing a number of individual car dealerships, as well as six Chevrolet dealer associations (large groups of dealers in one defined market area), when I got a call that turned out to be a game changer. The call was from Jerry Brown, whom I had met three years earlier when he was part of the Tampa Bay-area Chevrolet Dealers Association. Jerry was now the general manager of a Toyota dealership in Concord, North Carolina, and one of ten Toyota dealers in the Charlotte market. He asked if I wanted to come up to Asheville's historic Grove Park Inn to meet his fellow Toyota dealers, where they would be getting together for dinner and a meeting. I, of course, jumped at the chance, knowing that if I could build a relationship with this dealer group, we might eventually end up doing business together.

Several weeks later, I arrived at the Grove Park Inn just in time for dinner with all the Toyota dealers. Early into the evening, one of the dealers casually asked me if anyone else had come up from my office. I remember thinking what an odd question that was. Well, it turned out to not be an odd question at all, because after further conversation, I realized that the whole reason for this Toyota get-together was for the group to pick a new advertising agency the following morning.

This was clearly one of life's "OMG" moments, and I was terrified. There were three other agencies making presentations for this seven-figure account, and they would all be dressed in their Sunday best, armed with storyboards, market research, preliminary media buys, custom creative, and in some cases, nice little parting gifts for each of the dealers. I, on the other hand, was armed with business cards and an agency promotional videotape on VHS (remember those?). My intimate knowledge of Charlotte was that it was a city in North Carolina, and if I were to be given a Toyota product knowledge test that evening, my grade would've been a big fat *zero*! My first thought was to get through dinner, establish some relationships for further possible business, then notify the powers that be the next morning that, due to the circumstances, I'd regrettably have to withdraw from consideration.

It wasn't an early evening, and when I got to my room I couldn't go to sleep. "What an opportunity," I thought, and now I had to go back to Tampa with my tail between my legs. This account was big on many fronts. Yes, the budget was big, but more importantly, Saatchi and Saatchi, the billion-dollar agency that represented Toyota nationally, as well as all Toyota associations throughout the Southeast region, were not there to pitch. And, because this big powerhouse agency was not invited to the dance, it meant that one of the four regional groups would not only get the business, but they also would be sitting in the catbird seat if/when the other Southeast Toyota association went looking for a new agency. As I lay on the bed, in a woe-is-me moment, I started to convince myself that there was no way I could cop out without at least making an appearance at my scheduled time slot, which happened to be last. The longer I lay there, the more positive I became, convincing myself that even though I didn't formerly prepare for this pitch like I normally would have, I had in fact been preparing for this type of opportunity for over ten years. As far-fetched as it may have been at the time, in less than an hour, I had convinced myself that I could actually win the account. One big advantage was that I had had the opportunity to bond and build relationships with the dealers the night before at dinner. That was huge because I knew that I wouldn't be a stranger to anyone when I walked into that meeting room the following day.

The next morning, as I was checking out the room to make sure there was a VHS machine and a monitor, I ran into one of the other agencies that was to go on first. Their team consisted of three guys dressed in their Brooks Brothers best, all armed with portfolios, videos, and presentation books. I spoke briefly with the agency president, who pretty much dismissed my presence by wishing me luck with all the sincerity of Eddie Haskell from *Leave*

It to Beaver. I waited around for almost three hours until it was my turn at bat.

When I entered the room, it was like Old Home Week. "Hey, Cody!" one of the dealers called out. "It was fun last night!" Almost everyone greeted me like I had known them for years. Then, there I was, standing alone in front of the group, ready to give the pitch of my life. Now, make no mistake, while I had not done my normal research, and I had no spec creative to show, I knew the retail automobile business like the back of my hand. I didn't have a media presentation strategy for them, but I did know our agency strategy, which included negotiating annual buys, securing added value (additional media weight at no charge in consideration for paid media placed), post-buy analyses (making sure the stations delivered the right amount of gross rating points during scheduled flights), and our fifteen-second bookend strategy. I spoke at length about our creative strategy, which included hitting the right tone with the right message, as well as my idea on how the group should brand itself.

I finished the presentation with my coined "C Strategy," which is just as relevant today as it was twenty-five years ago. The "C Strategy" went like this: I slowed down quite a bit, looked everyone in the eye, and talked about the importance of commitment, consistency, continuity, and closing. I ended with a sincere *thank you* and told them that I would be honored to represent their group. They applauded, which is always a very good sign!

One thing about car dealers is that they don't take a long time to make decisions. Less than thirty minutes after I had finished my presentation, one of them came out to bring me back into the meeting room, where they congratulated me on winning the account. Wow! And to think I had almost walked away, given the circumstances. There is no doubt that having an opportunity to bond with the dealers the night before was a big advantage, but my biggest advantage that day was having the confidence, the ability, and the years of platform experience behind me. The other agencies, with all their people, all their research, and all their time and effort, were simply outgunned.

What happened next is almost storybook. Within four months of us taking over our new account, the Super 10 Toyota Dealers' market share went up by almost four points, prompting Southeast Toyota Marketing Manager Tony Stromberg to reach out and set up Toyota dealer presentations for other groups. In less than a year, we added an additional three associations to our agency's roster, and in the three years that followed, we represented almost half of the Toyota associations throughout the Southeast.

Make no mistake, I am a firm believer in being overly prepared whenever you have to make a formal presentation in front of a group, so in this instance, I was very lucky. But forging relationships always helps, and many of the dealers that were in the room that day have remained some of my closest friends, including Jerry, Joe Bertolami and the president of the association, Scott Clark.

A bit of advice: no matter how many times you've given the same speech, never, ever try to wing it! Just recently, I was in Florida at a ribbon-cutting ceremony for a new $30 million dealership for one of America's top automotive brands. These events are usually attended by local dignitaries, the *Who's Who* in the area, loyal customers, and always someone at a high level with the manufacturer. In this case, representing the manufacturer was the general manager of North American operations. This event was held outside, under a huge tent. There were about a hundred people, with the speakers seated in the front alongside the microphone and podium. First, the mayor spoke with his notes in hand, directing his remarks around the financial impact this store would have on the community. Then the owner, also with notes, thanked everyone for being there, as well as a long list of people responsible for the overall success and building of the new dealership. As the mayor and the owner were speaking, I could see this VIP from the manufacturer (and really the star of the event) waiting his turn with no visible notes. When he was introduced, up he came, full of energy and enthusiasm, thanking the dealer for his commitment to the brand. Then, with a smooth segue into the manufacturer's stump speech that he had obviously given many times before, he had a serious and what had to be an embarrassing lapse of memory. He proclaimed boldly that the brand stood for three things. He went on to explain number one, then number two (great so far), and with the level of excitement rising in his voice, "Number three…" Then dead silence. I felt his pain, as did everyone present. While he managed to squirm his way out of it, the whole mishap could have easily been avoided with just a little preparation. *Never, ever* try to wing it!

The great American modern dancer and choreographer Martha Graham, also known as the "Picasso of dance," knew the value of practice. Whether for dancing or speaking, her words about the necessity of practice for perfecting any performance are worth noting: "I believe that we learn by practice. Whether it means to learn to dance by practicing or to learn to live by practicing living, the principles are the same. In each, it is the performance of a dedicated precise set of acts, physical or intellectual, from which comes shape of achievement, a sense of one's being, a satisfaction of spirit. One becomes, in some area, an athlete of God. Practice means to perform, over and over again in the face of all obstacles, some act of vision, of faith, of desire. Practice is a means of inviting the perfection desired."

The longest I had ever prepared for an event was ten months when I was asked to officiate what *Weddings Illustrated* magazine referred to as "a fairytale romance and wedding." On Christmas of 2013, I was approached by two of my favorite millennials, Jacque

Cairone and Chris Gannon. Chris actually worked for me in the advertising business, but at the time had just made the decision to enter the restaurant business with his father, Tim Gannon, co-founder of Outback Steakhouse, one of America's most successful casual dining restaurant chains.

Tim was a food guru with a magic touch, who put together Outback's menus and original recipes, including his world famous Bloomin' Onion. He and I are lifelong friends; we were raised around the corner from each other, both in fatherless homes. With his big Irish grin and that twinkle in his eye, Tim can *schmooze* with the best of us.

That December day, and much to my surprise (because we didn't exchange gifts), Chris and Jacque greeted me with a very pricey bottle of Cabernet Sauvignon. "Wow! What's this?" I asked. They then told me that they had set a date for their wedding, and they wanted yours truly to officiate. Now that took me by surprise. While I have been asked to do every imaginable type of speaking situation, this was a first. I was honored but not quick to accept. I wanted to know why they had chosen me. And that's when they conveyed that they had felt a closeness and a bond to me. Plus, they knew I would bring some levity to the ceremony that they desperately wanted. They went on to say that because they didn't consider themselves religious, it would be hypocritical to have a member of the clergy preside over the wedding. Well, I accepted and started jotting down notes on how I might approach this unique speaking gig that very night. There were some things I had to consider. First and foremost, this would be a very special moment in their lives, and there was no way I was going to turn it into the *Cody Lowry Show*. Yes, I could deliver a humorous twenty-minute dialogue that would have everyone laughing, but to me, even though Jacque and Chris did not consider themselves religious, I just felt that setting the tone with a little reverence, laced with occasional and appropriate humor, was the way to go. I also respected the fact that there would be a large contingency of Catholics in attendance, including two of Chris's aunts who were nuns.

This was not going to be your average wedding, but rather one of Palm Beach's social weddings of the year, to be held at one of the world's largest polo clubs, the International Polo Club Palm Beach in Wellington, Florida. This was the perfect venue, since both Tim and Chris were champion polo players. Tim had won three U.S. Open Polo Championships and was inducted into the Museum of Polo and the Hall of Fame in 2013, while his son Chris, at the ripe old age of eighteen, helped his team win the U.S. Open Polo Championship in 2001.

Now, I didn't spend every waking hour over the next ten months working on my remarks, but I can tell you that because of the importance I had put on Chris and Jacque's special day, hardly a week went by when I didn't pull out the Gannon wedding folder to work on the presentation. Over the course of the summer and into fall, I reached out to Jacque, keeping her in the loop so she would be comfortable with the direction the ceremony was taking. One thing that I struggled with was the word "consummate" as well as the phrase "make it all legal," both of which were in a poem that I wrote and was to read. I am a firm believer that there is never a good reason to resort to profanity, or in this case, cross over into a gray area to get a laugh. When I say *struggle*, I mean *struggle*. One thing I knew for sure was that I didn't want those nuns taking a ruler to my knuckles if I crossed the line. About a week to go before the wedding, I made the decision to leave "consummate" and "make it all legal" in the poem. I think the right decision was made. What do you think?

The Beautiful October Wedding of Jacque and Chris

Today is your day,

Jacque and Chris,

The family and friends

All here for the bliss.

Yes, today is the big day,

You both look so regal.

The moment has come

To make it all legal.

You're both a bit nervous

Because it's all in the now,

In a matter of moments

You'll be saying your vows.

After the music

When it's getting real late,

Chris will whisper to Jacque…

It's time to consummate.

Around the corner…

Just a matter of time,

Everything will seem normal,

Incredibly fine.

Then Jacque will snuggle,

Giving her man a kiss.

It's time to get ready

For a little Chris.

Many years from now

When fatter won't matter,

You'll remember tonight

And all that's in sight.

The family…

The friends…

It was not to be missed,

The beautiful October wedding

Of Jacque and Chris!

As far as I know, everyone really liked the poem and, yes, I did manage to weave in some religious thoughts. Because the symbol for the wedding was a feather, and every wedding invitation included a beautiful feather, I decided to use that as a way to include the Big Guy Upstairs. Those close to Jacque and Chris knew this was a tribute to Chris being Chief Osceola, who along with his horse Renegade, were the official mascots at Florida State University. Since 1978, before each home football game Chief Osceola and Renegade have galloped onto the field in full Seminole garb and planted a burning spear with the force of a real warrior in the middle of the field. So, this is what I said:

> "We are gathered here this evening in the presence of a Higher Power to join Jacque and Chris on this very special occasion as they pledge themselves to one another. And, although this is their night, it's also your night and a tribute to all of you. Both family and friends have been a big part of their lives

and you helped to mold them into the two beautiful people they are today.

"Last December, Jacque and Chris honored me by asking me to be part of this very special ceremony. Well, you could have knocked me over with a… feather! Several months ago, when you received your invitation from Jacque and Chris, enclosed was a very simple, yet beautiful, feather that symbolizes the theme of tonight's occasion. The feather for tonight's special event symbolizes an ascension, a spiritual evolution to a higher plane.

"In Christianity, feathers have represented the virtues of faith, hope, and charity. In earlier times, Native Americans would pay homage to the Feather Sun, a symbol and cornerstone of their existence. It is my guess that the famous Seminole, Osceola— who was actually of Creek, Scottish, English, and Irish descent—would have also been mindful of the symbolism of the feather. And like Osceola, our groom this evening, Christopher, is a fearless warrior in his own right. On a horse…in the air… in the ocean, this warrior is gregarious, genuine, terribly inquisitive, and has never met a stranger in any walk of life. Jacque, the fairest feather of them all…beautiful, with a keen intellect, a contagious smile that lights up any room, and a sense of humor that allows her to keep up with the best of them.

"And so tonight, the marriage of Jacque and Chris becomes a symbol unto its own…a spiritual evolution to a higher plane."

One thing was for sure—my diligent preparation for this special event was not in vain. Everyone gave me rave reviews, and to this day, whenever I have an opportunity to be with Chris's father, Tim, he never fails to compliment me on the great job.

The Takeaway

The greatest gift you can give yourself, your children, and your grandchildren is being able to stand up in front of any audience and have a positive impact. And the best news of all—you don't have to be a child prodigy, because anyone with the right preparation, practice, and desire can do just that. Sure, it's going to take a little courage to get started, but just remember what the great Babe Ruth said: "Never let the fear of striking out keep you from playing the game."

Chapter Ten

SCHMOOZE ESSENTIALS

"Since your final destiny has yet to be determined,
why not make it extraordinary and leave
a lasting legacy?"

—MR. KEATING, *Dead Poets Society*

That's all, folks! That phrase was made popular by the Warner Brothers' classic Looney Tunes cartoons when Porky Pig would show up on the end scene proclaiming, "Th-th-th-that's all, folks!" Well, it's *not* over, folks, because this book would not be complete without some parting thoughts on the essentials of *schmoozing*.

There is no doubt that anyone reading this book knows someone in their family or circle of friends who is a stone-cold *schmoozer*. Maybe a boss or someone you work with. Perhaps a member of the clergy, an uncle, or an aunt. They have that *schmooze* gene, and it shows. In this book, I've endeavored to redefine the word *schmooze*, and to share with you some personal, real-life experiences and life lessons that have been immensely helpful for me during a business career that has spanned almost five decades. So, here are the ten basic tenets of *schmooze* that you need to keep in mind:

Have Fun

In 1983, Cyndi Lauper recorded the song "Girls Just Want to Have Fun." It was a runaway hit, reaching number two on the U.S. Billboard Hot 100 chart and becoming a worldwide hit over the next two years. Sure, girls just want to have fun, but the reality is that almost everyone wants to have fun and *should* have fun, regardless of age or gender. Along with diet and exercise, having fun should be part of every life coach's repertoire. The experts will tell you that having fun reduces stress, boosts energy, and improves your ability to cope. It'll even help you sleep more soundly at night. For me, I don't have to be on the golf course or off on some faraway vacation to have fun. People who know me will tell you that I am *always* having fun, and while some of the time it's with family, friends, and fellow associates, most of the time it's with total strangers that I meet when I'm on the road.

If you're traveling by air and you hear a dog barking, or see flight attendants laughing, I might just be on that plane. I fly almost every week, and I take great joy in making every moment count by interacting and having fun with fellow travelers and total strangers I meet along the way.

It's how I am no matter where I go. Several years ago, I was attending a Christmas dinner at the Citrus Club in Orlando, hosted by my friends, Walt and Pam Jennier. A group of about twenty of us were waiting for our table when the *maître d'* took our host aside and told him that they had to "cut me off." Cut me off? That was funny, considering I hadn't had the first drink! Look, I know everyone wasn't born with a lamp shade on his head, but you can still make a conscious decision to start each day with a little laughter in your life. Remember, if you live to be a hundred, life is still short, so have fun!

Be a Pushover

Yeager Airport in Charleston, West Virginia, is ranked as one of the top-ten worst airports in the nation, according to Frommer. com. It earns this distinction because of its "perilous location" atop a flattened hill that drops off three hundred feet on all sides. My wife's family on her mother's side is from West Virginia, so when our kids were young, we visited there. My wife Phyllis, five-year-old Cody Jr., four-year-old Chelsea, three-year-old Kipp, and I spent a week getting acquainted with our West Virginia side of the family. On the late afternoon of our scheduled flight home, the conditions got a little dicey, as heavy fog settled in and flights were canceled, including ours.

After checking into a hotel in the downtown area of Charleston, we headed to a Mexican restaurant within walking distance from where we were staying for a quick bite. As the family was almost to the restaurant, I was approached by a rather scary guy who was looking for a handout. Today, it seems like whatever city you go to, homeless people, or those just down on their luck, are actively working the streets for a handout. As common as that is today, thirty-three years ago, I had never been approached by anyone on the street looking for money. So, I waved him off and tried to hurry the little ones along. That's when he grabbed me from behind on the shoulder, asking once again for some money. Fearing for my family, I turned around and let this guy have it, telling him to back off or I was going to get the police.

As the family got settled inside the restaurant and was getting ready to order, I couldn't stop thinking about that guy, wondering just how bad off he was and wishing that I had handled the situation a little differently. I told my wife that I was going outside to try and find him. Who knows…maybe he was hungry? I remember it like it was yesterday. I gave my watch and my wallet to Phyllis, thinking that if I did get in some sort of trouble, the most I could lose was maybe the fifty bucks I had in my pocket, and off I went.

It wasn't snowing that night, but it was pretty cold, and as I walked up one block and down another, I finally found my guy. He was sitting on a park bench with what I later found out was his girlfriend. They were huddled together and obviously very cold. When I walked up to the couple, he was a bit startled at first. I immediately apologized for my defensive and combative behavior earlier and asked if they were hungry. They both nodded their heads. "Well, come on then. Let's find something to eat," I said. I was thinking of taking them back to the Mexican diner when he suggested a McDonald's just across the street. When we got up to the counter, his girlfriend turned around, as if to ask me what she could order. "Go ahead…whatever you want," I said. With that, she stepped up to the counter and ordered two Big Macs, fries, two apple pies, and a drink. At first, I thought she had ordered for both of them, but then he stepped up to the counter and said, "I'll take the same." Wow! Four Big Macs with fries and four apple pies. That may have been their only meal of the day.

Panhandlers in the USA have reached epidemic proportions, so I try and give something to anyone who is out on the street asking for help. Because of this, I've been labeled by some friends as a big pushover. I'll admit that it's hard to pass by these street people and not contribute to their daily take, even though I know I'm getting duped by some of them. But, when you consider that the largest percentage of panhandlers use their daily funds for food, it's hard for me to figure out just who the imposters are. So, go ahead, be a pushover!

Dazzle 'Em

I don't care what business you're in, when it comes to customer service, we should all follow the lead of Chick-fil-A. Would it surprise you to know that Chick-fil-A makes more per restaurant than McDonald's, Subway, and Starbucks combined? And, it's closed on Sundays. Would it also surprise you to know that, according to the 2018 ACSI (American Customer Service Index) survey, Chick-fil-A ranked number one when compared to eighteen other fast food chains? Chick-fil-A employees are trained to have a positive influence on all who come in contact with the restaurant. President and COO Dan Cathy said, "We strive to treat people better than the place down the street. One way we do this is by remembering that we are all people with a lot of emotional things going on that don't necessarily show on the surface, so we try to offer amenities and kindness that minister to the heart." At Chick-fil-A, it's all about their "customer first" approach to service. A staff member is always around to refill drinks, grab extra napkins, and to see if there's anything they can do to help. At the end of each order, the clerk behind the counter will routinely say, "It's been a pleasure to serve you," with a sincere and warm smile.

For my entire career in the advertising business, I have relied on great customer service to set us apart from the competition. In the automotive advertising world, retaining clients for more than ten years would be considered a job well done. Our company has clients on the books that have been with us for fifteen, twenty, and even thirty years. I credit that Herculean, almost-unheard-of tenure to incredible customer service. Early on, I instinctively followed a three-step process: build the relationship, get them to trust you, and never ever let the client down. Over the years, my relationships have evolved to almost family status with many of these clients. I'm invited to weddings and other specials events. When I'm in town, many insist that I stay at their house instead of a local hotel.

One *schmooze* tactic that I have deployed over the last twenty-five years is the annual Christmas gift. Rather than giving these multimillionaire dealers cigars, wine, or fine scotch, as they receive from so many of their vendors, I will send to each one's house, with their wife's name included on the card, a substantial Christmas flower or plant arrangement. The dealers' significant others absolutely love the arrangements and most of the time will let me know how much they loved my thoughtfulness. Here's one thank-you note:

> Dear Cody,
>
> Much belated thanks for the festive holiday arrangement. We enjoyed it in three stages over several weeks: as delivered, downsized and rearranged after the short-lived flowers faded, and recycled when the evergreen pieces were repurposed in a succeeding arrangement. The gift that keeps on giving! TMI? I just wanted you to know that your gift and you were appreciated throughout the holiday season. Looking forward to visits with you in 2018.
>
> Fondly,
>
> C. York

When it comes to customer service, dazzle 'em!

Get Through It

How many times have we heard someone say, "Get over it"? While on the surface that may seem to be good advice, it has a ring of flippancy that doesn't always fit. People who have suffered catastrophic or extremely unfortunate circumstances in their own lives may never "get over it," but they do get *through* it. As tough and as dysfunctional as my early years were, you could fill a football stadium with true stories of people who had it a lot worse than I could ever imagine. The key to overcoming adversity is pretty simple: keep a stiff upper lip and don't stop charging.

On January 7, 1993, at 12:30 a.m., Warrick Dunn, a football standout at Florida State University and an eventual first-round 1997 draft pick of the Tampa Bay Buccaneers, received a phone call that would change his life. His mother had been shot while working off-duty as a police officer for the Baton Rouge Police Department. At the age of thirty-six, Betty Dunn Smothers was pronounced dead, leaving the responsibility of raising five underage children to her oldest son, eighteen-year-old Warrick. At this point in his life, Warrick could have put his tail between his legs and run off to Florida State and lived the life of the football star he was sure to be. Instead, this young man, just out of high school, became the father figure to his five younger brothers and sisters. Using the $89,000 insurance money from his mother's death, Warrick purchased the first home the family had ever owned. And for the next four years, Warrick would travel from Tallahassee to Baton Rouge on weekends, holidays, and summer breaks to be with his grandmother and five younger siblings. Warrick will never get over that fateful day in 1993 when he lost his mother, but he did get through it, and today Warrick Dunn Charities has awarded 159 homes to single parents and their 420 dependent family members. No one is devoid of adversity in their life, and I, for one, am convinced that if we stay focused and stay positive, it will only make us stronger. Get over it? Maybe not, but we can get through it!

Laugh at Yourself

Raising three teenagers can bring out the worst in you, especially if you're trying your best to be serious in a situation that demands no less than a firm, authoritative father figure. My wife and I had just purchased what I thought at the time was the most beautiful couch we had ever owned. I say "at the time" because today my taste has evolved, and I probably wouldn't succumb to a wave of emotion and excitement at the thought of owning an emerald-green suede couch. Because this couch was the focal point of our living room, I couldn't help but admire that exquisite piece of furniture every time I walked into the room.

It was a sense of arrival for me, so you can only imagine my horror when one night I came home from work (my new prized possession only six days old) and there in the middle of the couch was a giant, dark stain. How could this be? Was this some sort of a joke? How could anybody be so cruel? The longer I looked at that stain on my new couch, the madder I got. Fortunately, before I drove myself to a complete out-of-body experience, I decided that I, the master of the house, would damn well get to the bottom of it.

I yelled to my three teenagers who were all downstairs at the time, "Cody, Chelsea, Kipp...get up here right now!" Up they came with expressions of terror on their faces, surely thinking that someone must have died (for me it was almost worse than that). There they stood at attention, ready for the sovereign leader's inquisition. "Look at this stain," I said. "I want to know who did this. I want to know now, and I want the *truth*!" With the same words and tone that Jack Nicholson delivered in the movie *A Few Good Men*, my oldest son Cody snapped back, "Dad, you can't handle the truth!" Well, I started to laugh and couldn't stop. All of a sudden, this supreme leader had lost his power to discipline. Today, whenever I think of that moment and how young Cody brought me back to reality, I always get a good laugh.

Similarly, there are many times in business when I've had to laugh at myself because of the way I was handling a situation. One such instance occurred in Kalamazoo, Michigan, a great town with a population of about 75,000, equidistant (150 miles) between Detroit and Chicago. Home to Western Michigan University and the original Gibson Guitar Company, it's also home to one of my many moments in life when I had to sit back and have a good laugh at myself. I had a trip scheduled to Kalamazoo and made a reservation at the Radisson Plaza Hotel. This hotel, owned by the Stryker family, founders of Stryker Corporation, one of the world's leading orthopedic and medical technology companies, is one of my favorites for many reasons. One is their incredible service. It's the kind of service you might expect if you were staying at the original Ritz in Paris, ranked as one of the most luxurious hotels in the world.

When I made my reservation two weeks prior, I also made a reservation at Webster's Prime, a five-star restaurant located on the top floor of the hotel, where, if you're up to the challenge and feel like splurging, you can order a twenty-two-ounce USDA Prime Cowboy Ribeye for $89. When I got to the hotel the afternoon of my arrival, I decided to head upstairs so that I might confirm my reservation, as well as see where my party might be sitting. I was greeted at the front desk of the restaurant and was told that my reservation had been moved from the main dining room to the less formal pub-like room across the hall. I had made this reservation two weeks ago and now they wanted to change venues? "No way," I said. Very politely, the young lady informed me they had a party that was taking up the entire dining room, and that they had tried to reach out to me to no avail. That wasn't good enough. I was steaming, and I demanded to see the manager in charge. My adrenaline was on the rise, and I was ready to give this guy a piece of my mind when from out of the kitchen came the person in charge, who happened to be the chef. Much to my surprise, *he* was a *she*, standing no more than five feet tall. With a glowing smile and dressed in her starched white chef coat, Tiffany Sawyer looked like a cover girl for *Bon Appetit* magazine.

Tiffany had poise that matched her grace, and with her immediate take-charge style, I was put on notice that she was not afraid of the big bad wolf. "What seems to be the problem, Mr. Lowry?" she said in a tone reserved for a child. Almost immediately, this atrocity that had been thrust upon me began to dissipate, making me wonder why I was making such a fuss at all. Resolving any issues that I had, she directed me to a table in the adjoining pub, with a promised round of drinks for my party. I was smiling and, yes, laughing a bit at myself, as well as Tiffany's ease of diffusing the situation. The next time you are taking *thyself* a little too seriously, go immediately to "Time-Out," count to ten, take a big breath, and laugh at yourself.

Pay a Compliment

Anyone who considers themselves a *bona fide schmoozer* knows that the fastest way to bring a great big smile to anyone's face is to pay them a compliment. For many of us, we become so self-absorbed in our own little world that we sometimes forget to recognize the incredible people around us who make our lives better than they might otherwise be without them. Think about the total strangers we meet along the way who give us incredible service. When was the last time you paid a waiter or waitress a compliment when they gave you extraordinary service? Sure, we leave a gratuity, but that's a sign of appreciation, not a compliment, and I can assure you even a generous tip pales in comparison to the feeling one will get when you look them right in the eye and deliver a sincere compliment: "John, the only thing better than the food was your great service."

Because of my hectic travel schedule, I feel like Hartsfield-Jackson Atlanta Airport is where I spend a good part of my life. As I connect to various cities around the country, I would be remiss if I didn't single out a special person while we're on the topic of compliments. Popeyes Louisiana Kitchen, located on Concourse B between Gates 13 and 14, is not just home to great chicken (I like the spicy), but also the second home to an elderly gentleman (I say "second home" because it seems like he is always there) who, in my opinion, has the people skills to be the head doorman at the Plaza Hotel in New York City. He is absolutely amazing to watch as he goes through his routine tasks at lighting speed—greeting customers, clearing tables, delivering food—all wrapped up with a personality and an attitude that summons a compliment from me whenever I'm fortunate to be in his company.

Compliments should be a genuine response to someone who has delivered a service or has performed beyond your expectations. John M. Gottman, PhD and author of *Why Marriages Succeed or Fail*, states that in good marriages, compliments outnumber criticism by more than five to one. So, whether it's service-related, positive feedback in the workforce, or part of your daily arsenal, compliments should be the gift that keeps on giving. And here's the best news of all: compliments are free, so pay a compliment!

Pay Attention to Your Brand

What does "brand" mean to you? For most of us, we immediately think of some pretty big names—Apple, Google, Amazon, McDonald's. What most people don't know is that a company's brand value is directly proportional to the public's perception and the goodwill associated with that brand. And while it may be difficult to measure the full value of a high-quality global brand, corporations know that the stronger the brand, the stronger the margins. Consider for a moment the estimated brand value in 2018 of some of these big global iconic names:

1. Apple: Annual Revenue = $229.23 billion; Brand Value = $214.48 billion

2. Google: Annual Revenue = $110.86 billion; Brand Value = $155.50 billion

3. Amazon: Annual Revenue = $177.87 billion; Brand Value = $100.76 billion

4. Microsoft: Annual Revenue = $89.95 billion; Brand Value = $92.72 billion

Coca-Cola came in at number five. Coca-Cola products are consumed at a rate of 1.9 billion drinks per day, had an annual revenue in 2018 of $35.41 billion, and an estimated brand value of $66.34 billion—almost *double* its revenue.

So, what's your personal brand value? Former Chief Executive Marketing Officer for Coca-Cola Sergio Zyman says, "Everything your company does and says at any given moment, down to the tiniest detail, either subtracts or adds to the value of your company." The same is true for our own personal brand. Everything we do and say at any given moment, down to the tiniest detail, either subtracts or adds to the value of our brand.

When it comes to building and establishing your personal brand, perhaps nothing is more important than a first impression. In a 1966 Madison Avenue advertising campaign for Botany Suits, the slogan "You never get a second chance to make a first impression" was created. How true! Human beings are programmed to size each other up quickly. Psychologists tell us that we have seven to thirty seconds to make that first great impression. First impressions have the ability to make or break our future relationships with potential clients, a new employer, or possibly a group of people to whom you're making a pitch or business presentation. How about remembering this catchy little acronym (thought of it all by myself) the next time you're making that first impression: SPDC.

1. Smile. Nothing takes the edge off and eliminates stress more than a winning and confident smile when making a first impression.

2. Prepare. If you're in a job interview, don't just know a little about that company, know a lot. If your meeting is with the president or CEO, do your homework. Know the college clubs they were in, the charities they contribute to—all the valuable information that may be helpful in that first meeting.

3. Dress for success. We've all heard the saying, and nothing could be truer. While today's business climate is more casual than it was twenty years ago, it's no excuse to take a casual approach to the way you look. A rule that I've lived by that has served me well: When in doubt, remember that you can never overdress.

4. Cell Phones. When it comes to negative use of cell phones, millennials have taken a bum rap for all of us. The fact is that all generations are addicted to their phones to one extent or another. From the time we wake up in the morning to the time we lay our head on the pillow at night, our trusted "blankie" is at our side. When making that first impression, do yourself a favor—turn the phone off and put it away!

A butcher, a baker, a candlestick maker…your personal brand is much more than positioning yourself within your own chosen profession. Building your brand is about how others value your character, your honesty and integrity, and maybe most importantly, your trustworthiness. People trust you when their experience with you consistently meets or exceeds their expectations. Remember, your personal brand isn't determined by what you think it is, it's determined by the people with whom you interact every day. Family, friends, co-workers, clients…that will be their call. Jeff Bezos, founder of Amazon and the wealthiest person in the world, said, "Your brand is what people say about you when you're not in the room." Pay attention to your brand!

Stay Relevant

It's not often that I give advice to a self-made billionaire, but that's exactly what I did several years ago, and he actually took my advice. This very close friend of mine made his fortune in the pharmaceutical arena. We were sharing a glass of wine, overlooking the Atlantic Ocean from his home in the famed enclave of Kiawah Island, South Carolina, when he reminded me of my sage advice. As we were solving the world's problems, he happened to mention a conversation we had had about a year prior. "Cody," he said, "you said something to me about a year ago and I've thought a lot about it, and I think you were right." I couldn't remember the conversation that he was talking about, but he went on to say, "I asked you when you were going to retire, and you said that you weren't going to retire—that you wanted to be relevant. And I'm going to take your advice." The point I was making at the time is that I enjoy being in the game, and that the thought of hanging it up and playing golf five or six times a week had absolutely no appeal.

The late Ray Kroc once said, "When you're green, you're growing. When you're ripe, you rot." I couldn't agree more. Most research today suggests that slowing down and retiring may not be good for your health. "At first, there is a honeymoon period where people go on vacation and spend time with their grandchildren," says professor Karl Pillemer, a gerontologist at Cornell University, "but it wears off. In general, people who engage in organized work have higher age mortality." Pillemer also says, "Working leads to other outcomes that are beneficial." Today, people over one hundred are the fastest-growing demographic in the world, with many totally engaged in their careers, as well as pursuing lifelong dreams. Diana Nyad is a seventy-year-old author, journalist, motivational speaker, and long-distance swimmer, who at age sixty-four became the first person to swim from Cuba to Florida without the aid of a shark cage. That's 110 miles! Her message is this: One, we should never, ever give up. And two, you are never too old to chase your dreams.

It doesn't matter how old or young you are. It's important to stay relevant in whatever endeavor you're engaged in. I'm the father of three millennials, and while some of the advice I gave as they were growing up may have fallen on deaf ears, one message got through loud and clear: "Get up early…leave late." Because of the connectivity capabilities in today's world, and the fact that you can work from almost anywhere, I would probably change that advice to, "Get up early…work late." To compete at the highest level and capture the best positions, baby boomers had to work smarter and harder than their peers. Today is no different. If millennials want to compete at the highest level and capture the best positions, they have to work harder than their peers at staying relevant in the eyes of those who will make decisions regarding their successes in life. Stay relevant!

Never Stop Dreaming

You know what I like about dreaming? For me, it's not about the past and it's not about the present; it's always been about the future. Like many of you reading this book, there have been times in my life when all I had were my dreams—dreams of better times to come and dreams that took me on a journey of escape and wonderment. And some of those dreams actually came true. "Daydreaming is what makes us organized," says Eric Klinger, professor emeritus of psychology at the University of Minnesota. "We think of daydreams as scatterbrained and unfocused, but one of the functions of daydreaming is to keep your life's agenda in front of you; it reminds you of what's coming up, it rehearses new situations, plans the future, and scans past experiences so you can learn from them."

I think what's most important is that we dream beyond life's expectations for us, and that our dreams are realistic. One chance in fourteen million that you're going to win tonight's Powerball is *not* realistic. And finally, what good comes from dreaming big if we don't act on those dreams? The late Erma Bombeck, humorist, syndicated columnist, and bestselling author, who had no easy road to success in her own life, yet had the perseverance to not give up on her dreams, said quite succinctly, "There are people who put their dreams in a little box and say, 'Yes, I've got dreams, of course I've got dreams.' Then they put the box away and bring it out once in a while to look in it, and yep, they're still there. These are great dreams, but they never even get out of the box. It takes an uncommon amount of guts to put your dreams on the line, to hold them up and say, 'How good or how bad am I?' That's where courage comes in." Never stop dreaming!

Appreciate

Nineteenth century Irish poet and playwright Oscar Wilde was born into a wealthy Irish lace-curtain family. Educated at Oxford, Wilde became one of the world's most popular playwrights. Unfortunately, this incredibly gifted talent also lived a flamboyant, extravagant, and sometimes over-the-top life, dying destitute at the age of forty-six. Thinking about his dissolute life and behavior, he wrote, "I became the spendthrift of my own genius…. I forgot that every little action of the common day makes or unmakes character.' My goal for anyone reading this book is that you don't become the spendthrift of your own genius. Make every moment count. I believe that most of us use only a fraction of our God-given talents, and having a new methodology (road map) to unleash your full potential and navigate the minefields you encounter on a daily basis will enable you to lead a happier, more productive life.

Schmooze, as you now know, is more than idle chit-chat. In summary, it's about being comfortable in your own skin. It's about stepping up to the plate when challenges arise. It's about taking advantage of opportunities to make a difference in the lives of others. And, it's about being willing to set aside that "woe is me" attitude when faced with one of life's many land mines. Adversity in our lives is a given, and no one gets a hall pass.

There is an old Japanese proverb that's one of my favorites: Fall down seven times, get up eight. For all of those experiencing adversity or hardship, you are not alone. No matter how many times you get kicked to the curb, a new dawn is just around the corner when you get up, brush yourself off, and continue to charge. Smile often. Laugh a lot. Listen. Engage the lonely. Follow your dreams and reach for the stars.

Remember, regardless of your age, life is short, and it's meant to be lived and to be appreciated. Being the product of a dysfunctional, chaotic, and broken childhood where my only treasures and solace in life were my dreams, I am truly indebted to the Big Guy Upstairs for all that he has bestowed upon me. Because of that, I believe the following are fitting words to live by:

> "Appreciate everything. Appreciate it when you go out on the street and the light is green, appreciate it when someone gives you a small candy, appreciate every compliment you receive, appreciate the love that people give you, appreciate every breath that someone takes before they tell you something because they took it for you. Appreciate. Even the

bad things because there's no better thing than balance and balance doesn't exist without bad things. Appreciate your balance. Appreciate your life. Appreciate yourself."

—Author Unknown

Now, to quote Porky Pig, "That's all, folks!"

And…may the *Schmooze* be with you!

About the Author

Cody Lowry's unique perspective and matchless storytelling skills can be traced back to his riches to rags upbringing. The privileged childhood he was born into evaporated in the empty bottles his father drained. The most constant element of his youth was moving: 32 times in a seven-mile radius.

Cody's debutante mother did her best to raise four children on her own. Government support was scant, and Saint Vincent De Paul only visited on Christmas Day. Out of that childhood developed a man uniquely qualified to write this book.

Against all odds, Cody graduated from the University of South Florida with a degree in advertising and public relations. With no financial help and in just four short years, he worked his way through college. His version of an all-nighter was sleeping in his 10-year old Corvair. As he recalls, the old beater used more oil than gasoline. Fresh out of college, he spent the next several years working the club circuit as a stand-up comedian, culminating in an audition for Saturday Night Live. He paid the bills as an automotive executive and made a name for himself as "Phabulous Philbert", an on-air pitchman who sold more cars than most could possibly inventory.

In 1984, he founded Dynamedia, a full-service advertising agency which he subsequently sold in 2015 to The Intermark Group of Birmingham, Alabama. Today, Cody is President of Intermark's successful Automotive & Retail division. Entertainer, pitchman, advertising executive…if you were to interview 100 friends, as well as the total strangers he meets along the way, they would describe Cody as unique, authentic, genuine, and very funny. What most people may not immediately notice upon meeting Cody is that beneath the veneer (or should we say behind the lampshade over his head) is a guy with a big heart who truly cares about others. Why? Because Cody Lowry has walked the walk.